GCSE TYPEWRITING AND KEYBOARDING APPLICATIONS

Margaret Gane
Nadine Todd

LONGMAN
REVISE
GUIDES

Longman

LONGMAN REVISE GUIDES

SERIES EDITORS:
Geoff Black and Stuart Wall

TITLES AVAILABLE:
Art and Design
Biology
British and European History
Business Studies
CDT: – Design and Realisation
Chemistry
Computer Studies
Economics
English
English Literature
French
Geography
German
Home Economics
Integrated Humanities
Mathematics
Mathematics: Higher Level and Extension
Physics
Religious Studies
Science
Social and Economic History
Typewriting and Keyboarding Applications
World History

FORTHCOMING:
CDT: – Technology
Human Biology
Music

Longman Group UK Limited
Longman House, Burnt Mill, Harlow,
Essex CM20 2JE, England
and Associated Companies throughout the world.

First published 1989

British Library Cataloguing in Publication Data

Gane, Margaret
   Typewriting and keyboarding applications.
   1. Typing
   I. Title   II. Todd, Nadine
   652.3

   ISBN 0-582-05192-4

Produced by The Pen and Ink Book Company,
Huntingdon, Cambridgeshire

Set in 10/12pt Century Old Style

Printed and bound in Great Britain by
William Clowes Limited, Beccles and London

C O N T E N T S

EDITORS' PREFACE

Longman Revise Guides are written by experienced examiners and teachers, and aim to give you the best possible foundation for success in examinations and other modes of assessment. Examiners are well aware that the performance of many candidates falls well short of their true potential, and this series of books aims to remedy this, by encouraging thorough study and a full understanding of the concepts involved. The Revise Guides should be seen as course companions and study aids to be used throughout the year, not just for last minute revision.

Examiners are in no doubt that a structured approach in preparing for examinations and in presenting coursework can, together with hard work and diligent application, substantially improve performance.

The largely self-contained nature of each chapter gives the book a useful degree of flexibility. After starting with the opening general chapters on the background to the GCSE, and the syllabus coverage, all other chapters can be read selectively, in any order appropriate to the stage you have reached in your course.

We believe that this book, and the series as a whole, will help you establish a solid platform of basic knowledge and examination technique on which to build.

Geoff Black and Stuart Wall

ACKNOWLEDGEMENTS

We are indebted to the following Examination Groups for giving permission to reproduce questions and coursework assignments taken from examination papers. London and East Anglia Group; Midland Examining Group; Northern Examining Association; Southern Examining Group; and we are also grateful to the Royal Society of Arts.

The advice and hints given are entirely our responsibility, as are the answers and displays we have presented.

We are also indebted to, and would like to thank, our students, especially Ruth Bolderston and Fiona Gowring for providing some of the examples. We very much appreciate the invaluable assistance and advice given to us by our Title Adviser, Fred Thorne, and thank him for allowing us to reproduce some of his material in chapter 11. Our thanks are also due to our Series Editors, Geoff Black and Stuart Wall, for their encouragement and help.

Lastly we would like to thank our long-suffering families, without whose patience this book would not have appeared, and Nadine's husband, John, whose culinary delights sustained us during the longer periods of work.

THE EXAMINATIONS AND ASSESSED COURSEWORK

GENERAL CRITERIA

MAIN AIMS

COURSEWORK

ASSESSMENT OBJECTIVES

GRADES

GETTING STARTED

This chapter is designed to show the various examinations covered by this book and the topics which are common to the relevant syllabuses. The introduction of GCSE has meant a change in format for the traditional typewriting examinations. For instance, all GCSE examinations include an element of coursework; typewriting and allied examinations are no exception. In many cases the traditional typewriting examination has been extended to cover various keyboard applications such as word processing and audio-typewriting. In fact the whole area of communication through a keyboard is now referred to as **text processing**.

In common with all other subject syllabuses, the Examination Groups have to stipulate the standards which must be achieved for the award of particular grades in various text processing examinations.

ESSENTIAL PRINCIPLES

The National Criteria set out the general principles of the General Certificate of Secondary Education (GCSE). The examination is administered by six groups of Examining Boards:

- London and East Anglian Group (LEAG);
- Midland Examining Group (MEG);
- Northern Examining Association (NEA);
- Northern Ireland Schools Examinations Council (NISEC);
- Southern Examining Group (SEG);
- Welsh Joint Education Committee (WJEC).

1 > GENERAL CRITERIA

All syllabuses havè to be approved by the School Examinations and Assessment Council (SEAC) under either *Subject Specific* or *General Criteria*. Typewriting and allied commercial subjects are approved under 'General Criteria'. For this reason there is no central set of aims and objectives for the individual subjects. Instead, each group of boards offering an examination in this area publishes its *own* aims and objectives, although these have been approved by SEAC.

The SEAC, in consultation with the Examining Groups, keeps the National Criteria under review and individual boards review and up-dates their syllabuses periodically. It is important, therefore, to obtain a copy of the *current syllabus* of the examination for which you are preparing.

Most of the main examining groups offer a GCSE examination in Text Processing. As can be seen from Table 1.1, the London and East Anglian Group, Midland Examining Group and Northern Examining Association call the examination **Typewriting**. The Southern Examining Group offers Typewriting, with optional papers in Word Processing and Audio-typing, under the title **Keyboarding Applications**. The modular syllabus of this latter examination is run in conjunction with the Royal Society of Arts and offers cross-certification with RSA. This means that as each module is satisfactorily completed, a single subject RSA certificate is awarded. The collection of a sufficient number of these certificates leads to the award of the GCSE.

EXAMINING GROUP	COURSE TITLE
London and East Anglian Group (LEAG)	Typewriting
Midland Examining Group (MEG)	Typewriting
Northern Examining Association (NEA)	Typewriting
Southern Examining Group (SEG)	Keyboarding Applications
Southern Examining Group with RSA Examinations Board (SEG/RSA)	Keyboarding Applications (Modular) GCSE

Table 1.1 GCSE Examinations

2 > MAIN AIMS

Each Group sets out individual aims and assessment objectives in its syllabus, but some aims are common to all. For instance each refers to the development of keyboarding communication for personal and business use.

The encouragement and development of skills enabling the production of a variety of well-displayed, accurate material on a typewriter or other keyboard is also referred to.

Mention is made of the need for language development enabling the candidate to communicate effectively. This may include understanding new terms or concepts and an appreciation of the effects of technological change upon keyboard communication.

All the Groups point to the need for self-criticism in order to produce accurate work (in other words it is necessary to check all your output) and the ability to understand and follow instructions.

	LEAG	MEG	NEA	SEG	SEG/RSA
CHAPTER					
3 Keyboarding	✓	✓	✓	✓	✓
4 Typewriting	✓	✓	✓	✓	✓
5 Business communication	✓	✓	✓	✓	✓
6 Composition of business documents	✓	✓	✓	✓	✓
7 Business meetings	✓	✓	✓	✓	✓
8 Information sources Itineraries	✓	✓	✓	✓	✓
9 Audio typewriting	✓	✓	✓	✓	✓
10 Word processing				✓	✓
11 Putting it all together	✓	✓	✓	✓	✓

Table 1.2 GCSE Syllabus/Topic Chart

This book is designed to cover the main topic areas of the examinations outlined in Table 1.2. It will also be useful if you are following one of the Office Studies and Information Technology courses listed in Table 1.3, as they have a word processing module or an element of word processing in the syllabus.

EXAMINATION GROUP	COURSE TITLE
London and East Anglian Group (LEAG)	Office Technology and Communications
Midland Examining Group (MEG)	Office Studies and Information Processing
Northern Examining Association (NEA)	Information Technology Syllabus A Information Technology Syllabus B
Southern Examining Group with RSA Examinations Board (SEG/RSA)	Information Technology (Modular) GCSE

Table 1.3 GCSE Information Technology Examinations

3 › COURSEWORK

Apart from the SEG/RSA Keyboarding Applications (Modular) which is a little different from the other GCSE examinations, each syllabus covered by this book requires the candidate to sit an examination as well as produce coursework.

In common with all GCSE examinations, some of the assessment process will reflect work done outside the examination room – i.e. *Coursework*. Details of the ways in which the various groups assess your work are given in Table 1.4.

TITLE	FORMAT AND REGULATIONS	PERCENT OF MARKS	TIME (HOURS)
London and East Anglian Group (LEAG) Typewriting (T/W)	Paper 1: Typewriting tasks Section A: Production tasks 70% Section B: Composition tasks 20% Reduced to 80%	80%	2½
	Coursework: 2 prescribed assignments; 4 tasks in each.	20%	Total approx 5½
	Limited grade exam: Max C Grade		
Midland Examining Group (MEG) Typewriting (T/W)	Paper 1: 6 compulsory typewriting tasks	40%	2
	Paper 2: Typewriting tasks including an element of composition	40%	1½ Total approx 6
	Coursework: 4 practical in-tray assignments	20%	

TITLE	FORMAT AND REGULATIONS	PERCENT OF MARKS	TIME (HOURS)
Northern Examining Association (NEA) Typewriting (T/W)	Practical Paper: Compulsory set of 5–8 typewriting tasks including an element of composition	70%	2
	Coursework: Folder of 25 exercises completed on a keyboard, based on checklist of tasks supplied by NEA	30%	no time stipulated
	Limited grade exam: Max C Grade		
Southern Examining Group (SEG) Keyboarding Applications	Paper 1: Common Core paper; 6 typing tasks on any kind of keyboard	40%	2
	Paper 2; Option paper; Typewriting or Word processing or Audio-typewriting	40%	2
	Choice of 2 levels: Paper 2A: General level: For those eligible for the award of Grades C to G 6 tasks based on Section 1 of chosen option syllabus		
	Paper 2B: Extended level: For those eligible for the award of Grades A to E 6 tasks based on Sections 1 and 2 of chosen option syllabus		
	Paper 3: Centre-assessed coursework 4 assignments involving real or simulated situations	20%	Total approx 6
Southern Examining Group (SEG) in association with RSA Examinations Board (RSA) Keyboarding Applications (Modular) GCSE	Credit accumulation within 2 years of the course 8 modules: 1 Text Processing Theory & Applications (RSA)		
	2 Core Text Processing Skills (RSA)		1
	3 Typewriting Skills Stage I (RSA)		2
	4 Word Processing Stage I (RSA)		1½
	5 Audio Transcription Stage I (RSA)		1½
	6 Typewriting Skills Stage II (RSA)		1¼
	7 Word Processing Stage II (RSA) Part 1		1¼
	8 Audio Transcription Stage II (RSA)		1¼
	Module 1: Centre-assessed on coursework		
	Modules 2 to 8: Externally examined Plus optional Copy Typing Speed Tests (RSA) Computer Keyboard Skills Test (RSA)		

Table 1.4 The Examinations and Coursework

4 > ASSESSMENT OBJECTIVES

The object of all GCSE examinations is to enable candidates to *show* what they know, understand and can do. It is therefore only fair to allow some of the assessed work to be produced in a more relaxed atmosphere during the course when candidates are less likely to be troubled with 'examination nerves' or time limitations.

Because the examiners are interested in rewarding candidates for skills and knowledge acquired, rather than penalizing them for what they do not know, most marking is done *positively*. However, in practical exercises such as typewriting and word processing, an element of *negative* marking has to be used, since all typographical errors must be penalized.

Initial coursework marking is undertaken by the teacher and then moderated (checked) externally so that all candidates work can be brought into line.

The coursework requirements of the various boards and examinations are shown in Table 1.4.

5 > GRADES

Grade Descriptions for all GCSE examinations were approved by the Secondary Examinations Council (now called the School Examinations and Assessment Council – SEAC) and it is not surprising that they appear similar. They are intended to give a general indication of the standards of achievement expected to be shown by candidates awarded various grades.

In common with all GCSE subjects, grades are awarded on a seven-point scale, Grade A being the highest and Grade G being the lowest. Below Grade G there is an ungraded band.

In general, descriptions of Grades C and F only are given in the syllabus (see Fig 1.5). Obviously candidates awarded A or B grades will have produced work significantly above that of the Grade C candidates. Similarly, candidates not having attained the requisite standard for a Grade F award may be awarded a Grade G. Occasionally, a syllabus will contain a description of grades other than C or F (see Fig. 1.6).

It should be remembered that the grade awarded is a reflection of the extent to which the candidate has met the assessment objectives *overall* and it might conceal weakness in one aspect of the examination which is balanced by an above-average performance in some other.

In some examinations (SEG Keyboarding Applications for example) candidates may opt to take the *common paper* or the *extended level paper*. Your teacher will help you to make the choice, since he or she will know the standard required and your capabilities. It is wise to be guided by your teacher since if you choose the extended level paper and do badly, it may mean that you are not awarded any grade at all, whereas the common paper will allow you to gain Grades C to G. It is necessary to choose between the common and extended levels at the time of *entering* for the examination.

Although two examinations (LEAG Typewriting and NEA Typewriting) have grade limitations, it is hoped that these limitations will disappear within a year or two.

The best way to assess what standard is required for the award of particular grades is to look at some examples. Figures 1.5 and 1.6 present the grade descriptions for just two of the subjects covered by this book.

In general it can be seen that for:

GRADE C

A wide range of knowledge is required together with the ability to organise and carry out instructions.

Knowledge and understanding of a wide range of aspects from the syllabus is required. Candidates need to be able to communicate effectively, with clear expression and reasonably wide vocabulary, especially where an element of composition is included in the syllabus or where free response answers are required.

All candidates need to be able to handle numeric work. In the case of typewriting examinations, this is necessary for the effective and accurate display of tabular work in particular.

Obviously, in the case of machine skills, candidates are expected to work accurately, checking and neatly correcting all work produced on the typewriter or word processor.

However the demands are not quite so stringent for grade F.

GRADE F

Candidates are still required to carry out instructions and to check and correct their work, but a high level of machine proficiency is not required.

Although candidates should have covered the full syllabus, there may be areas in which a candidate has not performed too well or where knowledge or skill is limited.

In some cases one has to read carefully to see the different levels of demand expected for the Grade C and Grade F candidates. Look at the MEG typewriting grade descriptions, for instance.

SEG Keyboarding Applications gives us an indication of what is required for a Grade A. Notice that, in this case, a candidate is expected to give a high performance in several areas – 'high degree of accuracy', 'high degree of competence', 'wide vocabulary' etc.

Grade descriptions are provided to give a general indication of the standards of achievement likely to have been shown by candidates awarded particular grades. The grade awarded will depend in practice upon the extent to which the candidate has met the assessment objectives overall and it might conceal weakness in one aspect of the examination which is balanced by above average performance in some other.

Grade F

Candidates will normally have demonstrated ability to

a) produce accurate typewritten work from typed and printed sources covering aspects of the syllabus.
b) check their own typewritten work for errors and correct them.
c) proof read typed or printed drafts and correct marked errors before producing an amended version on the typewriter.
d) understand and carry out instructions given.
e) display work in accordance with accepted practice including some work which involves calculations.
f) apply a knowledge of typewriting theory and display to tasks requiring some selection and re-arrangement of material.
g) compose and produce on the typewriter original material from at least one source, using general vocabulary with some awareness of correct grammar, punctuation and spelling.

Grade C

Candidates will normally have demonstrated ability to

a) produce accurate typewritten work from a range of typed, handwritten and printed sources covering all aspects of the syllabus.
b) check their own typewritten work for errors and correct them neatly.
c) proof read typed, handwritten or printed drafts and correct marked and unmarked errors before producing an accurate amended version on the typewriter.
d) understand and carry out instructions given.
e) display work effectively, choosing appropriate stationery, in accordance with accepted practice, including work which involves calculations.
f) apply a knowledge of typewriting theory and display to tasks requiring selection and re-arrangement of material.
g) compose and produce on the typewriter original material from a variety of sources, using general vocabulary with some awareness of appropriate tone, correct grammar, punctuation and spelling.

Fig. 1.5 Midland Examining Group (MEG) Typewriting Grade Descriptions

Grade descriptions are provided to give a general indication of the standards of achievement likely to have been shown by candidates awarded particular grades. The grades awarded will depend upon the extent to which the candidate has met the Assessment Objectives overall and it might conceal weakness in one aspect of the examination which is balanced by above average performance in some other.

Grade F

Candidates will normally have demonstrated:

i) an ability to work systematically to produce comprehensible copy in terms of spacing, layout and spelling;
ii) some proficiency in the use of the keyboard;
iii) an ability to process information into a given framework;
iv) an ability to recall information of a first-hand experience.

Grade C

Candidates will normally have demonstrated:

i) an ability to work accurately with a good degree of competence and consistency in the use of accepted standards of spacing, layout and spelling;
ii) some capability in the organisation and display of material;
iii) a fair vocabulary and use of acceptable expression in free-response answers;
iv) an ability to recall knowledge of both first and second hand experience;
v) an ability to recall and understand knowledge of accepted procedures and layouts;
vi) an ability to process information into a partially provided format;
vii) an ability to handle numeric work.

Grade A

Candidates will normally have demonstrated:

i) an ability to work with a high degree of accuracy, linked with a high degree of competence and consistency in the use of accepted standards of spacing, layout and spelling.
ii) insight and originality in the organisation and display of material;
iii) a wide vocabulary and the use of correct expression with originality in free-response answers;
iv) an ability to recall and understand knowledge from both first and second hand experience;
v) an ability both to analyse and to synthesise information into new and different formats;
vi) an ability to process information into an original format;
vii) a high accuracy in the numeric components of the work.

Fig. 1.6 Southern Examining Group (SEG) Keyboarding Applications Grade Descriptions

CHAPTER 2

EXAMINATION AND ASSESSMENT TECHNIQUES

COURSEWORK ASSIGNMENTS

COURSEWORK – EXAM GROUP REQUIREMENTS

PREPARING FOR THE EXAMINATION

TAKING THE EXAMINATION

GETTING STARTED

As mentioned previously, all GCSE syllabuses require the candidate to present coursework. In this chapter we shall deal with the preparation and assessment of coursework. We shall also look at ways in which you can prepare for, and take, the actual examination.

Typewriting and keyboarding examinations are a little different from most other examinations since they are testing the practical application of skills. It is not possible, therefore, to leave revision until the last few weeks.

ESSENTIAL PRINCIPLES

1 **COURSEWORK ASSIGNMENTS**

As previously mentioned, **coursework** is an essential element of all GCSE examinations. The inclusion of coursework ensures that students receive *continuous assessment* of their work throughout the course. It shows a prospective employer that you have worked to a high standard at all times and have not merely revised for a week or so before the examination and performed well on that day.

In many subjects the student is left to make decisions about the topic of the coursework. In Typewriting and Keyboarding Applications it is a little different since the examiners are seeking to assess skill development, so the type of coursework to be undertaken is largely *prescribed* by the Groups. You need to be guided by your teacher in determining *what* should be included, *when* it should be produced and *how* it should be tackled. Where there is an element of choice, your teacher will know whether the topic or piece of work you have chosen is relevant to the syllabus, acceptable for submission and will show your ability in the subject to the full.

> **Be guided by your teacher**

Coursework weighting is currently 20% of the total marks for LEAG and MEG Typewriting GCSE and SEG Keyboarding Applications examinations, and 30% in the case of NEA Typewriting. However, these weightings may change when syllabuses are revised.

> **Obtain a copy of the current syllabus**

Coursework is initially marked by the teacher. It is then moderated by external moderators appointed by the Examining Groups, to ensure fairness, accuracy and comparability of standards throughout the whole entry. One major difference between coursework and the examination is that you will be allowed to use textbooks, folders of past work and any other resource material to assist you in producing the work. It is, therefore, not so much a test of what you know but how you can tackle a task and produce an accurate piece of work. Although the time to be allowed for each piece of coursework is set down in some cases, it is usually fairly flexible – unlike the examination papers which must be worked strictly in accordance with the fixed time allowance.

> **Of course, this final attempt which is submitted must be your own work**

Although an essential element of the GCSE examination, coursework topics can vary considerably from Group to Group. For instance, NEA Typewriting requires the candidate to submit a folder of 25 pieces of work representing different stages of skill development and knowledge of theory. There is no fixed timetable for the completion of such work, although it is presumed that the tasks will be completed throughout the course as various aspects of the skill are taught, for example in display work, tabulation, business letters and so on. So important is this aspect of the examination that the NEA syllabus states that if the candidate submits an incomplete folder of work he or she will not be given a grade. On the other hand, some Groups specify approximately when coursework has to be undertaken.

We shall now look at the coursework element of each of the Examining Groups in a little more detail and suggest ways in which you can tackle this essential part of the examination.

2 **COURSEWORK – EXAM GROUP REQUIREMENTS**

THE LONDON AND EAST ANGLIAN GROUP (LEAG)

The coursework element in this examination is prescribed in detail by the Group, which also issues a detailed marking scheme. In other words the coursework could well be described as eight mini-examinations.

In addition to this, the period during which the work must be completed is strictly laid down, so that all candidates should be at a similar stage of skill development when they work the various assignments.

There are two assignments (A and B) to be worked, each containing four tasks. Assignment A sets tasks of a practical nature whilst Assignment B is more likely to involve the student in tasks of a secretarial nature – using reference books and composing business documents in order to produce typewritten exercises. Two of the tasks in Assignment A must be completed in the first half of the fourth term of the two-year course, and two during the second half of that term. The four tasks in Assignment B are similarly completed – two in the first half and two in the second half of the fifth term of the course.

Each assignment is likely to be written around a theme, so it is important to read the instructions carefully and to put yourself in the position indicated, e.g. 'You work as Junior

Secretary to Mr. P. Thompson, Sales Manager of DIY Tools plc.' Always keep in mind who you work for, the name and address of your firm, the name of your immediate employer and other important people in the firm or clients of the firm. You will almost certainly be required to refer to this information in order to complete some of the tasks.

MIDLAND EXAMINING GROUP (MEG)

In this Group's Typewriting GCSE the coursework element involves four practical in tray assignments which must be designed, by the teacher, to meet certain of the assessment objectives which show the candidate can:

a) interpret information presented in a variety of forms and extract relevant material from it;

b) deal with items involving problem-solving, e.g. identification of errors or re-arranging and analysing material;

c) communicate ideas in a logical manner, using correct and appropriate language, through the medium of the typewriter.

As with all GCSE Typewriting examinations there is an element of composition.

It is expected that the teacher will set assignments which will show the student's ability to 'solve real or simulated problems which may occur in a typical office'.

The Group stipulates that the assignments shall be completed 'during the latter part of the course' and that each assignment should take 1 – 1½ hours and be marked out of 20 (a total of 80 marks for the four assignments). The Group also publishes criteria to enable teachers to grade each assignment according to the assessment objectives outlined above.

NORTHERN EXAMINING ASSOCIATION (NEA)

As previously mentioned, the coursework element here is designed to enable candidates to demonstrate knowledge and skills acquired during the course. To do this the candidate has to submit a folder of 25 pieces of work completed on a typewriter, or other equipment capable of producing a typed copy, e.g. a personal computer or word processor. The folder must contain a sample piece of work from each of a list of specified topics, which range from simple passages with main and sub-headings and numbered paragraphs, through to display work, tabulation, working from manuscript, business correspondence, documents used at meetings and the identification of errors. One task which is unique to this Group's examination involves the compiling of a personal letter from oral instructions.

There is no specific time limit for the individual exercises, indeed students may complete the tasks at any time and in any order and are allowed two attempts at each task.

As regards assessment, again the Group provides quite detailed criteria to be used by the teacher when marking the assignments. Maximum marks are given for the five assessment objectives which are as follows.

The candidate's ability to:

a) communicate appropriately, accurately and effectively using a keyboard; (0 – 20 marks)
b) carry out instructions for given tasks; (0 – 15 marks)
c) use space appropriately in the layout and presentation of material; (0 – 15 marks)
d) use language accurately and effectively in the composition of material; (0 – 5 marks)
e) edit material and make the necessary corrections (0 – 5 marks).

External candidates (those not studying at a recognised centre) must submit their coursework folders direct to the Group and are required to attend an interview with the moderator to discuss the work and the conditions under which it was completed.

SOUTHERN EXAMINING GROUP (SEG)

In the Keyboarding Applications examination, the candidate is required to complete four assignments involving real or simulated situations. These assignments can either be devised by the teacher, or selected from among the specimen assignments issued by the Group. The four assignments should together cover all the assessment objectives. These aim to assess a candidate's ability to:

1   operate the keyboard accurately with full use of machine operation and to produce reliable copy;

2   be effective when checking work for errors and consequently to correct these in an appropriate manner;

3   comprehend instructions, including oral and written, and carry them out in an accurate and efficient way;

4   demonstrate a thorough knowledge of theory and display, and to apply this knowledge to new and different situations;

5   be competent in the calculations relevant to all forms of display on stationery of differing sizes;

6   use general vocabulary to meet the demands of manuscript with an awareness of correct grammar, punctuation and spelling;

7   compose and present material in an acceptable form.

The Group stresses that the coursework should be integrated into the curriculum, and be spread over the final year of the course. The assignments should occupy a total of between five and six hours of supervised time, although additional time is permitted for preparation and research. You will not be given a copy of the assignment until the supervised session, but if you have to carry out research beforehand, your teacher is permitted to brief you, and give you sufficient information to help you undertake it.

The work you submit for assessment must be your own – you will be required to sign a declaration certifying this, which your teacher will then authenticate. If you do copy material from other sources, you are obliged to acknowledge your source.

Your work will be assessed according to a mark scheme laid down by the Group. Credit is given for your achievements, although a proportion of marks will be lost for inaccuracies.

We hope the preceding information has given you some idea of the necessity of submitting a good set of coursework assignments. During your course of study, keep your assignments or other coursework separate from your other work so that it does not become creased or 'dog-eared'. Although no marks will be given for an attractive folder, the examiner will expect the work to be submitted in a folder of some kind, assembled in chronological or topic order and be clearly identifiable as your work – with your name, your candidate number and centre number on the folder or cover sheet and on each piece of work.

Make sure that the individual pieces of work are held together in some way yet can easily be detached or laid flat to allow for marking or moderating.

Coursework is set to enable you to show how well you can perform when not under pressure of an examination situation. It can gain valuable marks towards your overall examination grade.

3 PREPARING FOR THE EXAMINATION

In Chapter 1, Table 1.4. shows the methods of assessment for each of the examinations. You will notice that the LEAG and NEA Typewriting GCSE examinations consist of just one examination paper. LEAG's examination is 2½ hours long and accounts for 80% of the examination and NEA's is 2 hours long and accounts for 70%.

The MEG GCSE Typewriting, unlike the examinations of LEAG and NEA, offers the full grade ranges of A – G and has two papers. Paper 1 is 2 hours long and accounts for 40% of the total marks and Paper 2 is of 1½ hours' duration and also carries a weighting of 40%.

The SEG Keyboarding Applications examination is a little different from the typewriting examinations in that you may enter at the general or extended level and can choose various options for the second paper. Paper 1 is a common core paper which allows for the work to be produced on any kind of keyboard. It is in the options section (Paper 2) that you must choose typewriting, audio-typewriting or word processing and decide to opt for the general level or the extended level.

In the SEG/RSA Keyboarding Applications (Modular) the different levels are shown in the candidate's option for RSA Stages I or II in their chosen element.

In all GCSE Typewriting examinations you can expect the first paper, or first section of the single paper, to be confined to practical typewriting tasks whilst the second part of the examination will include elements of composition. The questions are usually arranged so that they start with the easier tasks and progress upwards in degree of difficulty. Marks allocated for each question are given in the paper so it is as well to attempt the questions in the order you find easiest, having regard also for the mark weighting.

You will become familiar with these aspects of the various examinations as you work through the examples given in each chapter of this book, since a wide range of past questions from all the Groups' papers and coursework have been included.

As far as preparing for the actual examination is concerned, there is one thing to keep in mind – you cannot afford to waste time during the course and hope to 'cram' during the last few weeks. Apart from the fact that the coursework has to be completed *during* the course, typewriting and the related subjects are *skills* which need to be built up through practice. You would not expect to learn to play a musical instrument simply by looking at it or by reading the score; just as you need to practice playing a musical instrument on a regular basis, if you are to become an expert, so typewriting and keyboarding demand the same application.

Bearing all these points in mind, you should approach the examination day in the knowledge that you have worked hard, developed your skill and are now at the peak of your performance. Try to look upon the examination as a challenge, a chance to perform at your best by producing accurate well-displayed work. After all, if you have prepared properly you will not be asked to do anything you have not previously tackled. Remember, the examiner is looking for a chance to give you marks, not take them away!

Having said all this, we must emphasise the need for *revision*. There are many points of theory to be remembered – how to display letters and other documents, the meanings of various printers' proof correction signs, how to work out display and tabulation work quickly and accurately. And although nothing can replace practising on the equipment itself, there is plenty of revision you can do even without a typewriter or word processor.

Many candidates who have been taught touch-typing think that this element will be tested in the examination room. They think the examiner will be there watching all the time. Of course this is not the case but, as you will see in the next chapter, those who do not touch-type are likely to penalize themselves.

4 ▷ TAKING THE EXAMINATION

Here are a few hints to help you approach the examination with confidence:

1 Remember, you will be nervous on the day of the examination. You will have probably begun to overcome this through the coursework you will have completed. But this is a very practical skill and it is very easy for 'everything to go wrong', to be 'all fingers and thumbs'. Remember, the first exercise will be simple. It is purposely designed to allow you to settle down, so if you find you are making lots of silly mistakes, slow down for a minute or two, telling yourself you have been typing for a long time and can cope with the work. Your nerves will soon settle and your fingers will start to respond with swift and accurate movements.

2 Students often tend to start again as soon as they make a mistake. This can be a dangerous habit and might lead to your running out of paper, especially special stationery such as headed paper and forms.

   However, it is pointless to waste time completing an exercise when you can see, after a few lines, that you are going to be penalized for, say, not having the correct line spacing or margins or using the wrong paper. In that case it is best to restart afresh.

3 As with all examinations, the best advice to candidates is to keep a clear head and to avoid revising up to the very last minute. Have an early night before the day of the examination, and make sure you arrive early and with the correct equipment. In the case of a skills examination such as typewriting, it is essential to arrive in the examination room well before the start of the examination so that you can 'try out' your machine to ensure that it is functioning properly and has sufficient ribbon and correction tape in it. Remember that if the machine breaks down during the examination, the invigilator should be called immediately.

   The machine will be repaired or you will be given another machine and any time lost will be noted. Examiners always read such notes about machine faults and take them into consideration when marking your work. They also appreciate how unsettling it can be to have something go wrong with your machine in an examination.

The rest of this book is devoted to a detailed analysis of the work required to be covered for the various examinations. Once you have studied it, we hope you will have more confidence in tackling both your coursework and the examinations.

CHAPTER 3

GETTING STARTED

The QWERTY keyboard (named after the arrangement of keys on the third row), is the standard layout used on typewriters, computers and word processors. It is used internationally – apart from a few additional or relocated keys on some foreign language machines.

The testing of quick and accurate operations on this keyboard is the basis for most types of office skills examinations, especially Typewriting and Word Processing. The best method by which to operate the keyboard is by touch, that is, locating the keys without looking at them, leaving the eyes free to concentrate on the copy or the screen. Whilst it is true that you will not be tested on this subject in the actual examination, it is a fact that those operators who have to look at the keys whilst typing are more likely to make the mistake of missing out portions of the text from which they are copying, or of transposing letters, words or phrases.

You will almost certainly have been taught touch-typing and you are recommended to drill persistently to advance your speed and accuracy in this basic skill. However, before you can put this skill to good use, you must be familiar with some basic rules of layout and the use of extra characters. This chapter is concerned with a revision of these rules and sets out various styles acceptable to the Examination Groups. They are equally applicable whether the work is produced on a typewriter or word processor.

BASIC KEYBOARDING

SPACING AND LAYOUT

TYPES OF PARAGRAPH

SPACING AFTER PUNCTUATION

OPEN AND CLOSED PUNCTUATION

LINE-END DIVISIONS

FOURTH BANK AND EXTRA CHARACTERS

FIGURES, MEASUREMENTS AND NUMBERS

CONSISTENCY, PROOF READING AND CORRECTING ERRORS

ADVICE

ESSENTIAL PRINCIPLES

1 ▷ SPACING AND LAYOUT

SIZES OF PITCH

The two main **sizes of pitch** are elite (12 letters to 1″ or 25mm) and pica (10 letters to 1″ or 25mm). There is a smaller pitch which allows 15 letters to 1″ but it not advisable to use this for examination purposes. The size of pitch is essential information if you are to calculate the number of spaces available across a sheet of paper or to centralize your work.

As A4 *portrait* (narrower edge at top) paper is $8\frac{1}{4}$″ (210mm) wide, it follows that there are 99 spaces across the page for elite (12) pitch and 82 spaces for pica (10) pitch.

Whatever pitch is used there are always 6 lines to 1″ (25 mm) when measuring vertically.

As A5 paper is half the size of A4 it can be seen that when used portrait there are 70 (elite) and 58 (pica) spaces available across the page. All this information is summarized in Fig 3.1.

> Check your machine is set for the desired pitch

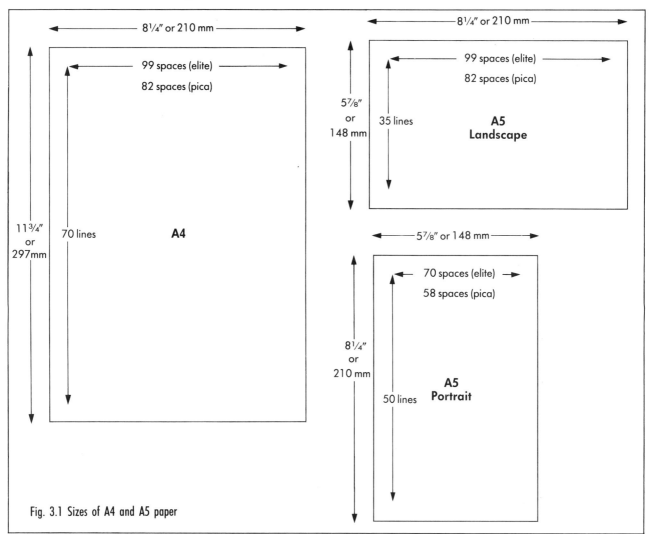

Fig. 3.1 Sizes of A4 and A5 paper

LINE SPACING

The most common **line spacings** are single and double. It is possible to substitute $1\frac{1}{2}$ line spacing for double on some occasions. Some typewriters are fitted with $2\frac{1}{2}$ or treble line spacing but this is seldom used unless typing a draft of work which is likely to be extensively revised.

Always check instructions to see whether the type of line spacing to be used is specified. If it is not, you are expected to choose appropriate line spacing.

Always leave a clear space between paragraphs **except** when using indented paragraphs and double line spacing. When using blocked paragraphs and double line spacing it is acceptable to turn up 3 or 4 single lines (leaving one or two clear spaces) between the paragraphs.

Blocked paragraphs are the most common

There are three types of paragraphs:

- **Blocked**: All lines begin at the left margin.
- **Indented**: When the first line begins ½″ (5 spaces pica or 6 elite) from the left margin. Most examining boards will accept 5 spaces for both pica and elite.
- **Hanging**: When the second and subsequent lines are indented 2 or 3 spaces from the left margin. Most boards will accept 2 spaces for both pica and elite machines.

There is more than one acceptable method of spacing after punctuation, but the method preferred by most boards is:

2 spaces after a full stop at end of sentence (also after question mark and exclamation mark);

1 space after colon, semi-colon or comma.

4 > **OPEN AND CLOSED PUNCTUATION**

This refers to the insertion of a full stop after abbreviations or at the ends of lines in an address. It will be dealt with in more detail in the chapter on letters. It is sufficient to mention here that in open punctuation there is no need to insert a full stop to denote abbreviations.

5 > **LINE-END DIVISIONS**

When using a word processor, or the more sophisticated electronic typewriters, there is no need to select a new line by using the carriage return at the end of a line. Line-ends are made automatically and whole words are carried to a new line. Such machines can also be set to justify the right margin.

However, on many typewriters it is still left to the typist to ensure that the right hand margin is kept as even as possible and it might, therefore, be necessary to divide a long word at the end of the line. In such cases the hyphen must be used at the end of the line, *never* at the beginning, and the division can only be made at certain points. The following is a list of the most common rules for division of words:

1 Always divide between two syllables, e.g. there-fore. Words of one syllable should not be divided.
2 Do not allow one letter to stand alone. Avoid leaving just two letters on one line.
3 In a hyphenated word, e.g. book-keeping, the division should be made at the hyphen.
4 A division can normally be made between double letters, e.g. dif-ficult.
5 Never divide items such as abbreviations, sets of figures, dates or proper nouns.

Whilst it is not so important to be able to touch-type these particular keys, they are very useful, not only for representing sets of figures but for many other signs and symbols.

We have already talked about using the hyphen key in hyphenated words or to divide a word at the end of a line. When a space is left before and after the hyphen it represents the dash. For example, I hope to go to town today – not tomorrow – to buy the up-to-date time-table.

COMBINATION CHARACTERS

When a character does not appear on the standard typewriter keyboard it can sometimes be made up by using two existing characters, e.g.

- **Division sign**   – hyphen, backspace, colon.   ÷
- **Exclamation mark** – apostrophe, backspace, fullstop.   !
- **Section**   – two superimposed s's or S's.   § §
- **Dagger**   – capital I, backspace, hyphen.   †
- **Double dagger**   – two superimposed I's or capital I and equals sign.   ‡ ‡

However, where foreign language accents cannot be satisfactorily made on the machine they should be inserted later with black biro or pen. This also applies to the plus sign, which, fortunately, now appears on most keyboards.

SUPERIOR AND INFERIOR CHARACTERS

In some cases a character needs to be slightly higher or lower than the writing. On a typewriter this is done by spacing up or down a half line-space. For example, H_2O; X^2; Marxism[1] or 46°F.

The latter can present some problems since there is a variety of acceptable spacing in the representation of degrees. Some boards allow any of the following:

18°C   18° C   or   18 ° C

Others, MEG for instance, insist that the space must be left before and after degrees sign. As few typewriters are equipped with the correct degrees sign, a lower case 'o' half a line space above the typing line is used.

FIGURES AND WORDS

You may produce all numbers as figures except where the figure begins a sentence. For example:

Three people were present.

MEASUREMENTS

Feet and inches can be represented by ' and ", or by typing the abbreviations ft and in. In the first case no space is left between the figure and the sign. In the latter one space is left. For example:

2′ 6″   **but**   2 ft 6 in

Similarly, a space is left before and after the multiplication sign:

210 mm × 297 mm

FRACTIONS

Not all fractions are represented on standard keyboards so a sloping fraction may have to be used. For example, 1/24 or 3/16. Where a sloping fraction is used it is advisable to represent all other fractions, occurring in that piece of work, as sloping fractions, e.g. 1/14 and 3/16.

PERCENTAGES

For percentages the figure is used followed either by the sign or the words per cent. For example, 45% or 45 per cent.

TIMES

The figure should be used followed by am or pm (open punctuation) or a.m. or p.m. (closed punctuation). For example:

10 am   2 pm   **or**   10 a.m.   2 p.m.

The 24-hour clock is now frequently used. This can be represented as:

1350 hours   **or**   1350 hrs (open) 1350 hrs. (closed)

TELEPHONE NUMBERS

A space should be left between the STD code and the subscriber's number. For example:

0942 654867

A hyphen is used only when there are two parts to the STD code:

01-879 4367

DATES

These should always be typed in full in the sequence day, month, year. Abbreviations such as 14-5-84 (acceptable in some countries) should not be used. There is more information concerning dates in the chapter on letters.

BRACKETS

When words or phrases are enclosed in brackets, no space is left before or after the word/s. For example:

(boys and girls) **not** (boys and girls)

A brace can be produced by vertical brackets:

(   )
(   )
(   )

8 ▷ CONSISTENCY, PROOF READING AND CORRECTING ERRORS

❝ The notion of 'consistency' is very important ❞

You will have noticed that, in many cases, there is more than one 'correct' or acceptable method. The Examination Groups appreciate this and ask only that you are **consistent** in the method you adopt. It would be unwise, for instance, to leave two spaces after a full stop at the end of a sentence for half the work and then change to leaving just one space, or to represent degrees as 16 ° C in one place then change to 16°C in another. Such inconsistency would be heavily penalized.

Just as important, from the examiner's point of view, is that you have taken the trouble to **check** your work. Proof-reading is extremely important, since work which contains errors is of little use in the business world. Hence all typewriting and word processing examiners expect you to produce 'mailable copy.' It is a good idea to check your work after each paragraph. Certainly it should be checked and corrected *before* it is taken from the typewriter, or if using a word processor, before it is printed. It is much easier to correct errors whilst the paper is still in the typewriter than after it has been removed, as this means a loss of time and also calls for expertise if the work is to be relocated properly.

You will be expected to correct **all** typographical errors. On some typewriters this can be time-consuming but, if expertly executed, you will incur no penalty. On manual typewriters or on most electric machines you will need to erase the error with a typing eraser, making sure you don't rub a hole in the paper. Alternatively, you may choose to use Tippex paper or correction fluid. In the latter case, make sure the fluid is not too thick and apply it lightly, waiting for it to dry thoroughly before typing over it.

Fortunately, most electronic machines have self-correcting devices which enable you simply to press the 'correct' key and retype the correct letter. Before the examination, ensure you have enough of the correct 'lift off' or 'cover up' tape in your machine and that this facility is working correctly. Remember, you need to use a lift off tape with a carbon ribbon and a cover up tape with a fabric ribbon.

EXAMINATION QUESTIONS

Task 1 This question was taken from the Specimen Paper 2 published by LEAG for their OTC (Office Technology and Communications) GCSE.

SECTION A *(42 marks)*

Candidates should answer all questions.

All answers to this Section should be completed on the question paper.

1

Look at the number	Tick box if it is the same	Enter the original number
1815	1815 ☐	☐☐☐☐
8972	8973 ☐	☐☐☐☐
1225	1229 ☐	☐☐☐☐
6069	6096 ☐	☐☐☐☐
1005	1005 ☐	☐☐☐☐

Look at the number	Tick box if it is the same	Enter the original number
9924	9924 ☐	⬜⬜⬜⬜
3319	3391 ☐	⬜⬜⬜⬜
442662	446262 ☐	⬜⬜⬜⬜⬜⬜
995594	999455 ☐	⬜⬜⬜⬜⬜⬜
233491	233491 ☐	⬜⬜⬜⬜⬜⬜
712245	712245 ☐	⬜⬜⬜⬜⬜⬜
606822	606288 ☐	⬜⬜⬜⬜⬜⬜
817108	816108 ☐	⬜⬜⬜⬜⬜⬜
936649	934449 ☐	⬜⬜⬜⬜⬜⬜
534210	543210 ☐	⬜⬜⬜⬜⬜⬜

Task 2   Although not an actual examination question, here is part of a typical piece of straight copy which might be used as the first question in a typewriting examination.

Type the following extract using double line spacing and suitable margins. Begin your typing at least 1″ (25 mm) from the top edge of the paper.

Several staff have complained recently about the lack of heating in the general office. It is noted that, according to the Health and Safety at Work Act, the minimum temperature should be 16°C (60.8°F), after the first hour of work.

It has been decided to keep a check on temperatures at the same time on successive days over the next week. Readings will commence on 23rd January, and end on 30th of that month.

You should take every opportunity to develop, not only the skill of accurate touch-typing, but also of expertly correcting errors, since you cannot expect to type for two hours (the average length of examinations) without making some mistakes.

THE THEMATIC APPROACH

You will notice that examination questions and coursework assignments often follow a theme. It is essential that you take time to read the preamble to the questions thoroughly. You may need to refer to information given here in order to ascertain names, addresses, dates etc, This will be evident as you work through other past examination questions used throughout the book.

You must also develop the habit of proof reading your work. In the LEAG Office Technology and Communications (OTC) examination, this aspect is actually tested.

Task 1   It might be a good idea to do this exercise and then get someone else to check your answers. It is not as easy as it looks.

Task 2   This appears to be a very straight-forward task but there are several extra characters involved and ample opportunity to make theoretical mistakes.

STUDENT ANSWER WITH EXAMINER COMMENTS

Look at the following student's attempt. At first glance there appear to be no typing errors but the examiner has managed to find a few.

Task 2

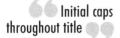Initial caps
throughout title

Several staff have complained recently about the lack of heating in

the general office. It is noted that, according to the Health and

Safety at work act, the minimum temperature should be 16°C (60.8° F),

after the first hour of work.

Inconsistent
spacing

It has been decided to keep a check on temperatures at the same time on

successive days over the next week. Readings will commence on 23rd

January and end on 30th of that month.

Do not divide dates at
the line end

USEFUL FOLLOW-UP WORK

Although not taken from specific examination papers, you might like to use the following to practise the specific keyboard skills referred to in this chapter.

EXERCISE 1

Using equal margins of 1″ (25 mm), type the following in double line spacing.

The Health and Safety at Work Act 1974 was brought into operation in stages commencing in January 1975. The Offices, Shops and Railway Premises Act of 1963 was already in operation.

The main aims of the new Act were to secure the health, safety and welfare of persons at work and to protect them against risks to health or safety arising out of, or in connection with, their activities at work.

The Act clearly set out the duties of the employer and of employees, pointing out that both had duties to ensure a safe working environment.

In the Offices, Shops and Railway Premises Act, provisions had been laid down to ensure adequate working space and temperatures. The Act clearly stated that there must be not less than 3.715 square metres (40 sq ft) of floor space for each worker – this to be inclusive of furniture and equipment.

A reasonable temperature must be provided and maintained in all rooms in which employees work (other than for short periods). A 'reasonable temperature' is defined as one which does not fall below 16 °C (60.8 °F) after the first hour of work.

Whilst the Act maintains that suitable and sufficient lighting must be provided, no specific standard is stated in this Act, with regard to the intensity of such light.

Most work places display notices about safety which invariably include the message to 'BE CONSCIOUS OF SAFETY AT ALL TIMES'.

Use double line spacing and suitable margins.

MEETINGS

If you join a local Youth Club you may be invited to become a member of the Committee which organises the Club. You may even be elected to a specific post such as that of Chairman, Secretary or Treasurer.

Working as a Committee Member, or in a specific capacity, can be time consuming and quite often arduous, yet it can be rewarding and give you valuable experience, not only in the conduct of meetings but in being able to 'get on with people'.

You will find that meetings are conducted in a fairly formal manner and so it is well to understand some of the Business Meeting Terms. Here are just a few of them.

AD HOC

The term literally means 'arranged for this purpose'. An ad hoc sub-committee is one which is appointed to carry out one particular piece of work e.g. arranging for a visit of a very important person (VIP).

CO-OPTED MEMBER

Such a member has been allowed to serve on a committee and is additional to the normal committee members allowed under the Constitution.

NEM CON (nemine contradicente)

This is the result of a vote in which nobody voted against the motion. It is not the same as a unanimous vote for a motion since in the case of a NEM CON result it means that some members have not voted – they have abstained.

There are many other terms to be understood if you are to take part in formal meetings. You are strongly advised to refer to a book on such matters. Your local reference librarian will assist you in your choice.

TYPEWRITING

SIMPLE COPYING

FORM FILLING

WORKING FROM MANUSCRIPT

DISPLAY AND TABULATION

REARRANGING MATERIAL

G E T T I N G   S T A R T E D

Most typewriting examination papers are structured so that you begin with relatively simple tasks and progress through to the more difficult. Throughout the paper you will be judged on your skill in operating the typewriter but in this chapter we shall look at favourite topics used by examiners to test your ability to interpret handwritten material intelligently and to display work effectively.

Any number of tasks may be presented in handwritten (manuscript) form, so it is wise to practise typing from several different styles of writing. By taking time to read through part of the task before commencing to type you will familiarize yourself with the characteristics of the writing, e.g. the different ways of forming specific letters. Be sure you know the standard abbreviations and printer's correction signs which may be used by the writer.

Manuscript work invariably includes some rearrangement of information. You should understand what has to be changed or inserted **before** you begin to type. You might like to remind yourself of such instructions by making a pencilled note on the question paper at the point where the rearrangement or insertion has to be made.

ESSENTIAL PRINCIPLES

1 SIMPLE COPYING

Almost all typewriting examinations begin with a relatively simple exercise, often straightforward **copying**. Where this is not the case, candidates are advised to spend at least ten minutes before the examination doing some keyboarding drills or copying practice. This not only helps to calm the nerves and get the fingers moving, but it provides a check that the machine is in good working order and that you are fully conversant with its features.

Begin by typing slowly and increase your speed as confidence grows and nerves relax.

As this will almost certainly be the first exercise the examiner marks, you want to make a good impression. The exercise should be error-free. Remember to check your work and correct all typographical errors **before** taking the work from your machine.

Here are a few hints for tackling this first question:

1   Make sure you read and follow instructions. The examiner may be testing your ability to use correct margins and to commence at a given point, e.g. to:

> "Start typing 2″ (50mm) from the top of the page."

This does not mean you turn up 12 lines (2″). If you do this you will be leaving less than 2″. Don't forget the line you need for typing on. So turn up **13** line spaces.

Remember the rules for line-end divisions

2   If the sizes of margins are given, make sure the paper is inserted at 'O'; otherwise your typing point will not be the same as the scale point. If you choose your own margins, see that the right-hand margin is not wider than the left and keep it as even as possible. This may mean dividing the occasional word at the end of the line.

3   Check whether line spacing has been indicated. If not, use your discretion. Although work should not be cramped into just half the available space, it is not necessary, in this instance, to plan work vertically with any degree of accuracy.

4   Check whether the type of paragraph to be used has been indicated. If not, it is wise to follow the type used in the draft, that is, in the question itself.

5   Remember that this is an exercise in which the examiner can check the accurate reproduction of various extra characters, e.g. the hyphen used in a hyphenated word and as a dash.

Now look at the examples of this type of question (Questions 1, 2 and 3) given at the end of this chapter.

2 FORM FILLING

There are many instances in the business world when you will be called upon to type information on to a **form**. It is for this reason that, in an examination, you may be presented with any one of a variety of printed forms and asked to complete it, using the typewriter, by inserting set information.

The most difficult part of this exercise is to use the interliner correctly. You need to practise this art, getting to know your particular typewriter:

1   When typing on a printed or dotted line make sure that the characters do not touch the line. They should be no more than 1 mm above the line.

2   Where you are given a rectangle in which to insert information, make sure the information is typed in the centre of the available space both vertically and horizontally.

Be consistent

3   If you need to sign the form or insert a character which is not on the typewriter (e.g. a tick), use a black pen.

4   Information on successive lines should be aligned vertically.

5   Make sensible use of available space. If you are given three printed lines for an address, don't type the whole address on the first line, leaving the rest blank.

6   If you are asked to 'Delete as appropriate', simply use the x key to overtype the printed words which are to be deleted. A small x is usually sufficient but you may need to use a capital X if the information is in block capitals.

7   It should go without saying that you must check that you are inserting all necessary information and putting it in the correct place.

Now turn to the end of this chapter and look at the questions presented on this topic.

WORKING FROM MANUSCRIPT

In the office situation a typist is often asked to work from a handwritten draft. This is called **working from manuscript**. Many of the exercises you will be required to type in the examination will be presented in this form.

Styles of handwriting vary considerably so it is useful to get as much practice as possible in this aspect of the subject. Work produced in manuscript form is often abbreviated and corrected by the writer, so the first thing to learn is the common abbreviations and printer's correction signs used by the printer. You will find the principal ones in these two boxes of key terms:

Abbreviations used in manuscript

a/c(s)	account(s)	or	other
ack	acknowledge	rec	receipt/receive
appt(s)	appointment(s)	ref	reference
bn	been	sec	secretary
bel	believe	sh	shall
cat(s)	catalogue(s)	shd	should
co	company	/ or t	the
dept	department	thro'	through
dr	dear	w	with
f	for	wd	would
ffy	faithfully	wh	which
fr	from	wl	will
hv	have	yr(s)	year(s)/your(s)
immed	immediately		
necy	necessary		

Printer's correction signs

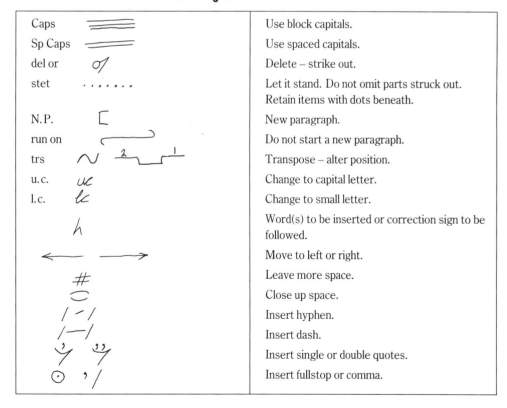

Caps		Use block capitals.
Sp Caps		Use spaced capitals.
del or		Delete – strike out.
stet		Let it stand. Do not omit parts struck out. Retain items with dots beneath.
N.P.		New paragraph.
run on		Do not start a new paragraph.
trs		Transpose – alter position.
u.c.		Change to capital letter.
l.c.		Change to small letter.
		Word(s) to be inserted or correction sign to be followed.
		Move to left or right.
		Leave more space.
		Close up space.
		Insert hyphen.
		Insert dash.
		Insert single or double quotes.
		Insert fullstop or comma.

These lists are not exhaustive but should form the basis of a resource which you can expand yourself. Before you begin typing:

1 Read through the passage, or at least part of it, so that you become familiar with the style of writing.
2 Put a circle around any word you do not understand and return to it when you have got the sense of the passage.

3 If you are not sure of the spelling or even the existence of a strange word, look it up in a dictionary. Examiners do not expect to correct 'jibberish'!

4 Make sure you understand all the corrections which have to be made **before** you commence to type. A failure to do this may result in your completing a long and complicated passage only to find that something should have been inserted earlier in the piece or that the order of things should have been changed.

5 When dealing with abbreviations, be sure you know which are accepted abbreviations and which have to be typed in full. For instance, 'co.' means 'company' but in the title of a firm it is always represented in its abbreviated form, i.e. Smith & Co. Ltd.

6 As you know, all work should be vertically placed on the paper. With continuous manuscript work it is difficult to judge the length of the piece, although this will come with practice. If in doubt, take the time to type just a few lines on a scrap of paper. You can then calculate how much of the handwritten work fits on to one typewritten line and so set suitable margins and line spacing.

Now look at the questions on this topic at the end of this chapter.

4 ▷ DISPLAY AND TABULATION

Although you may expect to have to type a tabulated statement and a piece of work requiring extensive display, the two elements are present in almost every exercise. Most work needs to be planned vertically and a short tabular statement could occur in a letter or memorandum.

RULES

Check with Chapter 3

The object of a specific test of tabulation or display is to ensure that you can set work out *precisely* in the centre both horizontally and vertically. This merely requires you to know the sizes of paper and type which you will be using (see Fig 3.1 on page 14). Here are a few more hints for tackling these questions.

1 Check whether you have been instructed about the *size* of paper to use. If not, the choice is yours, but remember a piece set neatly in the centre of a page with fair-sized margins all round looks better than something which spreads out across the whole sheet.

   Whilst A5 paper can be used with the widest edge at the top (landscape) or with the shortest edge at the top (portrait), A4 paper is usually used 'portrait'.

2 There are two types of layout, the *blocked* and *standard* methods. Most examination groups will accept the blocked method; indeed you might be instructed to use this method (see Question 1 at end of this chapter).

   The *blocked* method means that, although work is centralized vertically, only the longest line of a display piece is centralized horizontally. All other lines begin at the same point as the longest line.

   In *tabulated* work it means that columnar headings begin at the same point as the longest line of each column. In all cases, main and sub-headings should be typed against the left margin although occasionally you may be instructed to type a centralized heading over a blocked tabulated statement.

Watch out for specific instructions

3 Remember, main headings are usually typed in block (or spaced) capitals with or without underscore. Sub-headings may be typed in initial capitals. Two clear spaces should be left after headings before commencing the body of the work.

4 Where headings are typed in Block Capitals, either *one* or *two* spaces may be left between words. In Spaced Capitals, *three* spaces must be left between words. There should be no full stop after headings, unless the full stop has been used to denote an abbreviation.

Be consistent.

5 Underscoring on headings should begin with the first letter and end with the last. Do not underscore punctuation points at the end of headings. (This is particularly important when underscoring shoulder headings.) Underscoring should be directly under the typed words; do not turn up a line space before underscoring. It is not necessary to underscore more than once. A heading which has two, or three lines under it merely instructs you to type in block or spaced capitals – not to underscore two or three times.

See Key Terms – correction signs.

6 *Centralizing headings*: In the majority of cases headings which have to be centralized will be across work which has equal margins, hence it is necessary to find the middle of the paper and backspace **half** the number of letters and spaces in the heading.

Where the margins are unequal, e.g. 18 and 87 (elite), you need to add the two margins – 18 + 87 = 105 – and then divide by 2 to find the centre point of the writing line. You can then backspace in the usual way. If there are several headings to be centralized, it is a good idea to set a tab stop for the centre point, so that it can be quickly located on subsequent occasions.

Whatever you do, ensure that your paper gauge is set correctly at 'O', otherwise all your efforts at centring will be to no avail. Of course, many electronic typewriters have automatic centring devices.

7   Some display exercises require a *tailpiece*. This is simply a decoration usually at the end of the passage. You can make up your own decoration something like:

ooOoo   **or**   * * * * *   **or**   xxxXxxx

On a menu, this decoration may be used between courses, but do not overdo such work. Heavily decorated borders are time-consuming and, unless expertly executed, can cause loss of marks through typographical errors.

SPECIFIC RULES FOR TABULATION

8   There are several methods of calculating the point at which to set the margins and tab stops. Having calculated accurately, check that you set the machine correctly. Always type *across* the page, not down the columns.

9   Do not mix the standard and blocked layouts of tabulated statements. This is particularly important where there are columnar headings, for example:

STANDARD METHOD

Sales figures

Region	September	October	November
	£	£	£
Birmingham	950	1,500	1,650
Cardiff	2,320	2,100	1,970
Derby	1,540	2,010	2,160

BLOCKED METHOD

Sales figures

Region	September	October	November
	£	£	£
Birmingham	950	1,500	1,650
Cardiff	2,320	2,100	1,970
Derby	1,540	2,010	2,160

Notice, in the blocked method the only time figures do *not* commence at the same point is when they need to fall in alignment vertically – tens under tens, units under units, etc.

10   When typing 'thousands' you may either insert the comma (as in the example above) or leave a space after the thousand, e.g. 2 320. Don't mix the two methods in an exercise.

11   If a figure is omitted, you should type a hyphen in its place. One hyphen is usually sufficient, but be guided by the instructions in the exercise.

12   Rule the tabular statement only if instructed to do so and then keep to the lines as indicated in the draft. You may use the underscore on the typewriter or a black pen to draw the lines, or a mixture of both.

13   *Leader dots* are a succession of dots which help to carry the eye from one column to the next when reading the table. Use them only where there is sufficient space to warrant their use or where instructed to do so.

Leader dots can be typed in a variety of methods, e.g.

. . . . **or** .. .. **or** . . . . **or** . . . .

Whichever method you choose, see that there is *at least* one clear space after the last word, before starting the dots and stop the line a clear space from the end of the column. See that the dots fall in alignment vertically.

Now look at the questions on this topic at the end of this chapter.

5 REARRANGING MATERIAL

It has already been emphasized that both the examination paper and coursework for GCSE may be set around a theme. Hence you may be required to refer to other sections, tasks or questions to obtain relevant information to enable you to complete a set question.

In the sections on working from manuscript and tabulation it has also been seen that transpositions frequently have to be made or 'ballooned' sections inserted. Take care with such insertions. Ensure that they are made at *exactly* the right place in the text and that no punctuation points have been obscured by the arrow.

Additionally you may be required to completely re-arrange information, usually lists. You may be asked to 'type in numerical order'. This does not necessarily mean you need to type the *numbers*, merely put the items in order. You may be asked to type in descending or ascending order – perhaps the prices of property. You may be asked to rearrange material chronologically, that is in date order – usually with the earliest date at the beginning.

However, the most common form of arrangement is *alphabetical*. Here you need to know the basic rules for alphabetical indexing. You are probably aware of the fact that, in the case of names, you take the initial letter of the surname as your filing index letter. But do you know the following simple rules?

> **Some rules for alphabetical arrangement.**

1   Where several names begin with the same letter, look to the second or even third or fourth letter:

    e.g. Barton J
          Barton W
          Bowen
          Brown

2   Nothing comes before something. This rule means that where two names are almost identical the shorter precedes the longer:

    e.g. Brown
          Browne
          Browne G.

3   A firm consisting of several surnames is filed under the first of the names:

    e.g. White, Brown and Green Ltd.

4   Hyphenated words are filed under the first part of the name.

    e.g. Foster-Brown

5   When words begin with 'O' or with prefixes such as De, the prefix is treated as part of the name:

    e.g. D'Arcy
          De La Rue
          O'Farrell

6   Names beginning with 'Saint' however spelt (St. or Saint) are treated as Saint. The same applies to names beginning with M', Mc or Mac, all of which are treated as 'Mac'.

7   Names which include figures should be treated as though the figure is written in words:

    e.g. 6 Point Garage becomes Six Point Garage.

You will notice that it is customary to type lists of names with the surname first, followed by the forenames or initials and, where necessary, the title. 'The' to begin a company is placed at the end:

e.g. Universal Stores plc (The)
     White, J. (Mrs.)

Similar rules apply to government departments:

e.g. Health and Social Security, (Department of)

Now look at the questions on this topic at the end of this chapter.

EXAMINATION QUESTIONS

Let us look at some examples of questions which have been set on these areas of the syllabuses.

Question 1

Type the following passage on A4 paper, using double line spacing and the fully blocked style. Begin typing 1½in (about 40mm) from the top of the paper and use margins of 1in (25mm) on both the left and the right.   (LEAG; 1988)

```
Probably the most important purchase one makes in life, and certainly the most costly, is a
house. Insurance can help the house purchaser in many ways.


Firstly, the Building Society or other institution lending the money to finance the  purchase
will make it a condition of the loan that the building is insured. To ensure that the true
value of the house is covered, an index-linked policy is recommended.


Secondly, one should insure the contents of the house against loss or damage. Again it is
essential to consider the true cost of replacing any damaged items. A "New for Old" policy
would ensure that any item lost or damaged could be replaced, not merely with an item of
equal age and value, but by a new item.


Lastly, home owners taking out a mortgage with a Building  Society will wish to take out a
mortgage protection policy. This will ensure that, should the purchaser die before the full
amount borrowed has been repaid, the insurance company will pay the outstanding debt.
This type of policy is not necessary if the house is being purchased by way of an endowment
assurance policy.
```

Question 2

Type the following scene description in double line spacing on A5 portrait paper.
                                                                  (NEA; 1988)

```
'Candida' by Bernard Shaw

The scene is set in the drawing-room of St Dominic's
Parsonage.  The room has a large plate glass window
overlooking a park.  This is the room where the
Reverend Morrell does his work. When the curtains
open he is sitting in a revolving chair at the end of
a long table. [At the opposite end of the table is a
typewriter and his typist is sitting at this machine.
The table is littered with pamphlets, journals, letters,
an office diary and postal scales.
```

Question 3

Type the following letter using open punctuation in the fully-blocked style, using suitable margins and single line spacing, on a sheet of headed A5 paper (148 × 210mm). Take one carbon copy on the yellow paper provided. Insert today's date. Complete the reference with your own initials. Correctly address a C6 envelope.   (MEG; 1988)

```
PB/

Luxi-Tours Ltd
28 Ratcliffe Avenue
Nottingham
NG1 6DP

For the attention of Mr D Stephens

Dear Sir

We are hoping to organize a visit for our members
to a Weekend Wholefood Conference to be held at
Quorndale Hall in Leicestershire on 16 and 17 July
1988.

I should be grateful, therefore, if you could send
me your quotation for both 52 and 60 seater coaches
to transport our members to the Conference on
Saturday morning, returning to Nottingham on Sunday
evening.

Yours faithfully



Pauline Bradshaw (Mrs)
Secretary
Vegetarian Society
```

ADVICE AND COMMENTS: SIMPLE COPYING

Questions 1, 2 and 3

The first thing you notice in these three examples is the length of the questions. In Question 1 (LEAG) you are expected to type quite a lot so there is ample opportunity for you to make mistakes! The examiner is also testing your ability to use the fourth bank characters – notice the inverted commas in the third paragraph.

Question 2 (NEA), on the other hand, is particularly short although there is a correction sign to be followed.

The third question (MEG) is surely the most difficult of these first questions. Although you have a very short and simple letter to type, you are also asked to take a carbon copy and type an envelope. We all know how difficult and time-consuming it can be to have to correct errors on a carbon copy and you are certainly likely to make the odd typing error until you get into the swing of things.

FORM FILLING   ### Question 4

Complete the Early Booking Form for Miss Moira McLean who wishes to book 4 seats for the Tuesday performance. Her order of preference for seats is Front Circle, Stalls, Upper Circle, and her membership number is 842142. She will sign and date the form herself.

You will need to refer to Background Information and Question 2 above for some of the information.   (NEA; 1988)

To help you answer this question the relevant extra information required is presented below:

Miss Moira McLean
28 Church Road
Northchester
Lancashire
T66 2SP
Telephone number 0524 379801

The play, CANDIDA, will be performed for 6 evenings from Monday, 7 November, to Saturday, 12 November 1988, at the Northern Theatre, Northchester, commencing at 7.30 pm.

EARLY BOOKING FORM

FRIENDS OF THE NORTHCHESTER PLAYERS

NAME (Mr/Mrs/Miss/Ms)* _____

ADDRESS _____

_____

_____

TELEPHONE NUMBER _____

I wish to book _____ seats for the production of _____

on (DAY) _____

DATE _____

Please indicate in the boxes below your order of preference for seats by numbering 1, 2, 3.

☐   ☐   ☐
Stalls   Front Circle   Upper Circle

MEMBERSHIP NUMBER _____

SIGNED _____   DATE _____

* delete as appropriate

ADVICE AND COMMENTS: FORM FILLING

As examination papers and coursework assignments are often set around a theme, some information needed to complete one task has to be extracted from other parts of the examination paper. This is the case with this particular question.

You will notice you are required to insert a single figure in the middle of a box. This is difficult so make sure you practise the art well before the examination.

WORKING FROM MANUSCRIPT

Question 5

Type the following article on a suitable sheet of paper in single line spacing and change the style to the blocked style. Keep the hanging paragraphs in the lettered section, which should be inset in the new layout. Use a dictionary to correct any spelling errors.

(MEG; Specimen Paper)

> The Industrial Revolution — caps and underscore
>
> Raw Materials — caps-no underscore
>
>   Originally the Severn Valley Railway used to run under the town of Bridgnorth and through Coalbrookdale to join the line to Shrewsbury. At Bewdley museum an exhibition can be seen showing how charcoal was produced prior to using it in the smelting of iron ore. In 1709 Abraham Darby used a blast furnace at Coalbrookdale to become the first man to smelt iron using coke (made from coal) as a fuel instead of charcoal. It was the close proximaty of coal, iron ore, water (for power and transport), sand (for moulding cast iron), limestone (to flux the slag in the blast furnaces) and clay (for bricks and tiles) which enabled the area to become the cradle of the industrial revolution.
>
> Iron Smelting - caps-no underscore   EXOTHERMIC
>
>   The modern industrial manufacture of iron uses exothermic reaction which, in forming carbon monoxide, raises the temperiture of the furnace to 1500°C.
>
>   (i) Coke, limestone and iron ore are added to the furnaces and hot air is forced through.
>
>   (ii) The iron ore (Fe_2O_3) is reduced to molten iron.   CALCIUM
>
>   (iii) The heat decomposes the limestone ($CaCO_3$) to calcium oxide (CaO) which forms molten calcium silicate slag which has sandy impurities $CaO + SiO_2 = CaSiO_3$.
>
>   (iv) The slag is tapped off from the surface of the molten iron while the iron, which contains about 6% carbon, is cast into solid ingots of pig iron.

ADVICE AND COMMENTS: WORKING FROM MANUSCRIPT

At least the handwriting appears to be easy to read in this passage. However, it is full of place names and scientific terms, many of which may be unfamiliar to you, so read through carefully before commencing to type. The writer has assisted you in some cases by printing the word in a rectangle. Remember this does not mean that you have to type the word (exothermic or calcium) in block capitals. It is printed that way merely to ensure that you spell it correctly.

Watch out for the *inferior* and *superior* characters. These can become a little cramped when typing in single line spacing if you choose to move up or down half a line rather than using the interliner.

Another point to watch is the representation of *degrees*. You will recall that there are several methods of doing this – see Chapter 3. Some of the Examination Groups offer a guide to teachers as to what is, or is not, acceptable so I am sure you will have been told which form to use by the teacher preparing you.

Roman numerals can be a little 'tricky'. In fully-blocked work it is acceptable to align them at the left. In indented work it is better to align them at the right. The main passage had to be typed in fully-blocked style but the section numbered in this way was in a different layout.

You will notice that you have been left to choose 'a suitable sheet of paper'. There appears at first sight, to be quite a lot of words so I expect you will choose A4 but you will soon realize that you need fairly wide margins and must start quite some way from the top of the page. However, examiners would consider that this is more attractive than trying to fit it on to A5 paper which would mean using very narrow margins all round.

Lastly, did you spot the two *spelling errors*? They were 'proximity' and 'temperature'. If your spelling is not too good it will mean you have to check several words, but examiners usually test you on words which are commonly misspelled.

Be sure to study the Tutor's answer to this question.

DISPLAY AND TABULATION

Question 6

Using A5 paper (148 × 210mm), type the following menu in single line spacing, separating the course with a row of asterisks. Top/bottom margins should be equal and the longest line centred to the page.

(MEG; 1988)

M E N U — spaced caps

Celery Soup
Melon Cocktail
Stuffed Cucumber Rings
Fruit Juice
* * * *

Vegetable Lasagne with Cream Sauce
Mushroom Flan
Wholewheat Macaroni Cheese
Lentil Croquettes with parsley sauce
New Potatoes
Crisp Green Salad
* * * *

Rum and Raisin Cheesecake
Apricot Syllabub   [SYLLABUB]
Fruit Crumble and Cream
Cheese and Wholewheat Biscuits
* * * *

De-caffeinated Coffee

[DE-CAFFEINATED]

Question 7

Type a corrected copy of the following table on A4 paper setting it centrally, vertically and horizontally, on the sheet. Rule as indicated. Type the word PRODUCTION in spaced capitals as a main heading.

(LEAG; 1988)

The following are the production figures for the month of March 1988.

Region	Net Business	Target	Deviation
	£	£	£
Sheffield	29229	27000	1- 2229
Preston	21242	22000	- 2814
Liverpool	39650	37000	+ 2650
Manchester	33432	32000	+ 1432
Hull	17186	20000	- 758
Totals	140739	138000	+2739

ADVICE AND COMMENTS: DISPLAY AND TABULATION

Question 6

A menu is often set as a test of your ability to display work effectively. Since there are no set rules to follow, apart from seeking a balanced effect both vertically and horizontally, it is essential to read the instructions carefully to see if the examiner has made any specific demands.

Question 7

You can expect to be required to type at least one tabulated statement during the course of the examination. Such statements often require ruling. In this case only horizontal lines are needed so it will be easy to insert these on the typewriter.

REARRANGING MATERIAL

Question 8

Type this memorandum on A4 paper, addressed to The Conference Secretary from The General Manager. Use this reference:
AS/GR/4/17/OA.

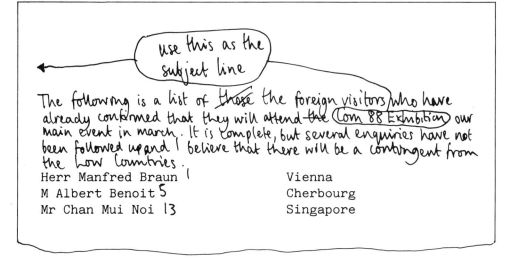

use this as the subject line

The following is a list of those the foreign visitors who have already confirmed that they will attend the Com 88 Exhibition our main event in march. It is complete, but several enquiries have not been followed up and I believe that there will be a contingent from the Low Countries.

```
Herr Manfred Braun  1              Vienna
M Albert Benoit 5                  Cherbourg
Mr Chan Mui Noi 13                 Singapore
```

```
    Sr  Pedro Gervas      9        Barcelona
    Mr  Hew Fong Chock    11       Hong Kong     Re-arrange in
    Herr Johann Kreuls    7        Zurich        the order 1-13
    Mr  Lai Wai Kiew      12       Hong Kong     but do not use
    Sr  Manuel Lopez      10       Madrid        those figures.
    M  Gustave Reynaud    6        Paris
    Herr George Schmidt   2        Bonn
    Herr Heinz Schwarz    3        Hanover
    Herr Heinrich Todt    4        Hamburg
    Herr Franz Weber      8        Berne
```

I ~~shall~~ (hotel) expect to give you the final draft before the end of the month when our list should have 18 to 20 names. Details of accommodation required for these visitors (and for the 50 or so who are coming from various centres in the U.K.) will be passed to you as soon as possible.

Question 9

The following letters, received in 1985, should be placed in alphabetical order by name.

Do not write out the list.

Place number 1 beside the letter which comes first, 2 besides the second one and so on.

No.	Name	Town	Date	Order No.
213	M. McKay	Catford	14.6.1985	
217	5 Star Laundry	St Neots	24 July	
256	Allstar Data Ltd	Sandy	14 July	
201	John Smith	Stevenage	16 June	
242	Model Machinery	Chelmsford	12 June	
273	J. O'Donnell	Romford	31 May	
223	J. Smith	Ampthill	30 July	
232	R. Stephens	St Albans	07.07.85	
235	M. MacAnders	Stamford	14.7.198	
236	J.C. Smithers	Stotfold	24 June	
215	Alison Aaron	Colchester	24.VII.85	
226	P. Stephenson	Colwyn Bay	5.V.85	
236	Waste Disposal	Saintsford	30 May	

ADVICE AND COMMENTS: REARRANGING MATERIAL

Question 8

This is a fairly straightforward task. Although you are asked to change the order, numbers have been used to indicate the order of the items. Remember the instructions not to type the actual figures.

Reading the instructions carefully, you will notice that this is a *memorandum*. It should be typed on the A4 memorandum form which will almost certainly be supplied with the question paper. Do not forget to include the date on the memo.

The writer's handwriting is not very clear, so you will need to read it through carefully before commencing.

Notice that there is a heading – **Com 88 Exhibition**   (LEAG; Specimen Paper)

Question 9

This question is not taken from a typewriting examination, so you are not required to type anything. We have included it to remind you that this is a popular test in many office skills' examination.

You might like to try this exercise for yourself. There are one or two quite 'tricky' names to watch out for, for instance McKay and MacAnders. Do you remember the rule which says that all names starting with M', Mc, or Mac are treated as though spelt Mac? And what about the name '5 Star Laundry'? Do you remember that names starting with numbers should be treated as though the number was written in full – Five Star Laundry?

(LEAG OTC; Specimen Paper)

A STUDENT'S ANSWER
TO QUESTIONS 1, 4, 6 AND 7
WITH EXAMINER COMMENTS

SIMPLE COPYING   Question 1

66 Typing errors should be noted and corrected immediately.

66 Less than 1½" 99

Probably the most important purchase one makes in life, and certainly the most

costly, is a house. Insurance can help the house purchaser in many ways.

66 Margin less than 1" 99

Firstly, the building Society or other institution lending the money to

finance the purchase will make it a condition of the loan that the building

is insured. To ensure that the true value of the house is covered, an index-

linked policy is recommended.

Secondly, one should insure the contents of the house against loss or damage.

Again it is essential to consider the true cost of replacing any damaged items.

A "New for Old" policy would ensure that any items lost or damaged could be

replaced, not merely with an item of equal age and value, but by a new item.

Lastly, home owners taking out a mortgage with a Building Society will wish

to take out a mortgage protection policy. This will ensure that, should the

purcheser die before the full amount borrowed has been repaid, the insurance

company will pay the outstanding dept. This type of policy is not necessery

if the house is being purchased by way of an endowment assurance policy.

66 Spelling or typing error? 99

66 Is this candidate touch-typing? 99

FORM FILLING   Question 4

EARLY BOOKING FORM

FRIENDS OF THE NORTHCHESTER PLAYERS

66 Use 'x' to delete. 99

NAME (Mr/Mrs/Miss/Ms)*   Moira McLean

ADDRESS   28 Church Road

Northchester

Lancashire

T66 2SP   66 Too high. 99

TELEPHONE NUMBER   0524 379801

I wish to book ___4___ seats for the production of ___CANDIDA___

on (DAY) ___Tuesday___

DATE ___8 November 1988___

Please indicate in the boxes below your order of preference for seats by
numbering 1, 2, 3.

66 The numbers should be
centred. 99

[2]   [1]   [3]
Stalls   Front Circle   Upper Circle

MEMBERSHIP NUMBER   842142

SIGNED   *Moira McLean*   DATE 11/5/88

* delete as appropriate

66 Instructions said form
should be left unsigned. 99

DISPLAY AND TABULATION

Question 6

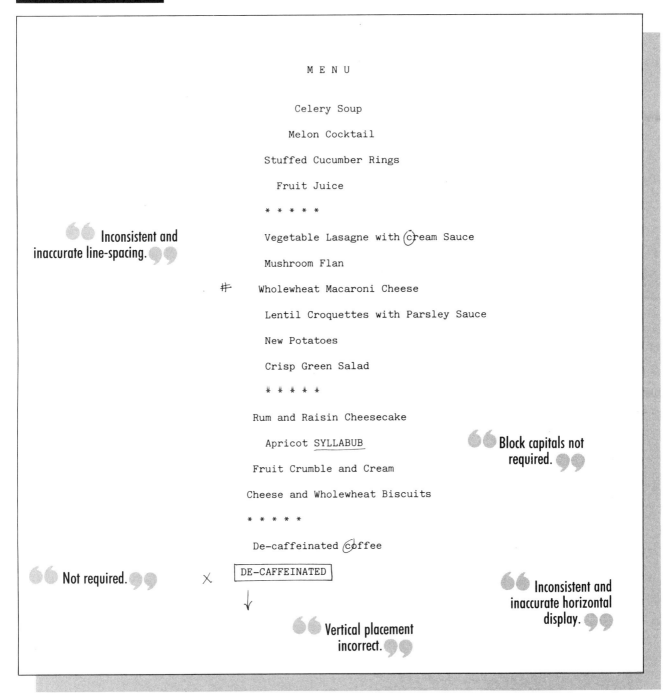

M E N U

Celery Soup

Melon Cocktail

Stuffed Cucumber Rings

Fruit Juice

* * * * *

Vegetable Lasagne with cream Sauce

Mushroom Flan

Wholewheat Macaroni Cheese

Lentil Croquettes with Parsley Sauce

New Potatoes

Crisp Green Salad

* * * * *

Rum and Raisin Cheesecake

Apricot SYLLABUB

Fruit Crumble and Cream

Cheese and Wholewheat Biscuits

* * * * *

De-caffeinated coffee

DE-CAFFEINATED

Inconsistent and inaccurate line-spacing.

Block capitals not required.

Not required.

Vertical placement incorrect.

Inconsistent and inaccurate horizontal display.

It is unlikely that the student read the instructions for this question since it was quite clearly stated that single line spacing should be used. In this case the student has attempted to type the whole exercise in double line spacing but probably without setting the line space regulator correctly since a space was missed between two items.

The blocked form of display was called for, as the instructions said 'the longest line centred to the page.' Had each line needed to be centred there would not necessarily have been a specific instruction to centre each line but rather an instruction merely to 'centre the work both horizontally and vertically.'

It is possible that this student was not sure which method to use and so started by centralizing each line and then, after the fourth item, attempted to follow the display in the the draft, commencing subsequent lines at the same point as the writer.

This student also did not realize that manuscript words printed clearly within a rectangle are to assist the typist in reading the word, not an instruction to type in block capitals.

One wonders if the two obvious typing errors ('cream' and 'coffee') are not further cases of inconsistency – this time in the use of initial capitals for the names of dishes.

Question 7

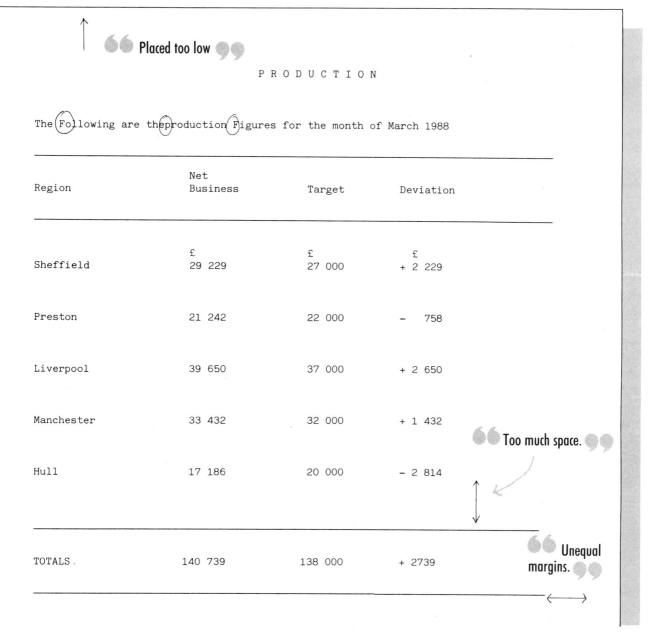

66 Placed too low 99

P R O D U C T I O N

The (Fo)llowing are the(p)roduction (F)igures for the month of March 1988

Region	Net Business	Target	Deviation
	£	£	£
Sheffield	29 229	27 000	+ 2 229
Preston	21 242	22 000	– 758
Liverpool	39 650	37 000	+ 2 650
Manchester	33 432	32 000	+ 1 432
Hull	17 186	20 000	– 2 814
TOTALS .	140 739	138 000	+ 2739

66 Too much space. 99

66 Unequal margins. 99

At first glance this appears to be quite a good attempt but a closer look reveals some quite important errors which will certainly be penalized.

Firstly, the outside margins are not equal – this means the work has not been centred horizontally.

Although quite a good attempt has been made at correct vertical placement it is placed a little too low on the page.

There were no specific instructions regarding the line spacing to be used, but one feels that to leave *four* clear line spaces between items, as this student has done, is spacing the work out excessively. Surely the table would have looked neater and more compact if double line spacing with equal outside margins had been used. Even within the table the spacing should be consistent. The space between the horizontal line and the £ sign should be the same as that between the last item and the horizontal line preceding the TOTALS LINE.

Now consider the typing errors in the first line. It is possible that the candidate mistook each of the writer's 'f's for a capital letter. They are not very clear but the student should know that capital letters would not be used for two words in the middle of a sentence, unless the words were Proper Nouns – as in March.

Although the student has correctly included the main heading 'PRODUCTION', it would have been better to type this against the *left* margin since the fully-blocked method of tabulation has been used.

A TUTOR'S ANSWER

WORKING FROM MANUSCRIPT

Question 5

THE INDUSTRIAL REVOLUTION

RAW MATERIALS

Originally the Severn Valley Railway used to run under the town of Bridgnorth and through Coalbrookdale to join the line to Shrewsbury. At Bewdley Museum an exhibition can be seen showing how charcoal was produced prior to using it in the smelting of iron ore. In 1709 Abraham Darby used a blast furnace at Coalbrookdale to become the first man to smelt iron using coke (made from coal) as a fuel instead of charcoal. It was the close proximity of coal, iron ore, water (for power and transport), sand (for moulding cast iron), limestone (to flux the slag in the blast furnaces) and clay (for bricks and tiles) which enabled the area to become the cradle of the industrial revolution.

IRON SMELTING

The modern industrial manufacture of iron uses exothermic reaction which, in forming carbon monoxide, raises the temperature of the furnace to 1500° C.

(i) Coke, limestone and iron ore are added to the furnace and hot air is forced through.

(ii) The iron ore (Fe_2O_3) is reduced to molten iron.

(iii) The heat decomposes the limestone ($CaCO_3$) to calcium oxide (CaO) which forms molten calcium silicate slag which has sandy impurities $CaO + SiO_2 = CaSiO_3$.

(iv) The slag is tapped off from the surface of the molten iron while the iron, which contains about 6% carbon, is cast into solid ingots of pig iron.

DISPLAY AND TABULATION

Question 6

```
          M E N U


          Celery Soup
          Melon Cocktail
          Stuffed Cucumber Rings
          Fruit Juice

          * * * * *

          Vegetable Lasagne with Cream Sauce
          Mushroom Flan
          Wholewheat Macaroni Cheese
          Lentil Croquettes with Parsley Sauce
          New Potatoes
          Crisp Green Salad

          * * * * *

          Rum and Raisin Cheesecake
          Apricot Syllabub
          Fruit Crumble and Cream
          Cheese and Wholewheat Biscuits

          * * * * *

          De-caffeinated Coffee
```

C O U R S E W O R K   A S S I G N M E N T S

Here are some examples of assignments on the same topics.

Again, remember that some information may have had to be extracted from another source. For example, in Task 3 the whole assignment revolved around The Villagers Amateur Dramatic Society, hence the heading should be typed in full – not as V A D S.

TASK 1

Complete the Booking Form for the new production. Fill in the name and address of the producer and the name of the Society. His business phone number is 0231-6790. The large hall with stage is required from 26 April 1988 to 30 April 1988, and the large meeting hall on 25 February and 3 March 1988. Thirty-six cups and saucers and fifty large plates are required on 26 April. Special lighting is required from 27 to 30 April. Date for tomorrow. Do not sign. Insert dashes where facilities are not required. (LEAG; 1988)

Castleton Leisure Centre

The Croft
Castleton
Norfolk NR13 2CT

BOOKING FORM

I wish to book the following facilities in the Leisure Centre

NAME OF APPLICANT _____

HOME ADDRESS _____

_____

TELEPHONE NUMBER (home) _____ (business) _____

NAME OF SOCIETY _____

MEETING FACILITIES

Large Hall (with stage)

Date(s) required _____

Large Meeting Hall

Date(s) required _____

Small Committee Room

(Date(s) required _____

OTHER FACILITIES

Hire of Crockery: _____ cups _____ saucers

_____ small plates _____ large plates
_____ wine glasses _____ tumblers

Date(s) required _____

Special Lighting (give date(s) required) _____

_____

I agree to pay for any damage or breakages.

Signed _____ Date _____

Note: In an *earlier task* the name and the address of the producer and the name of the Society were given:

Producer: Chris Davies
222 Ash Hall Road
Castleton
Norfolk NR7 2SR
Telephone: 0231-55780
Society: The Villagers Amateur Dramatic Society.

TASK 2

You are the school secretary and work in the office of Broadwater Middle School, Downside Road, Reading, Berks. RG12 3AH. Students and staff of the school are putting on a performance of the musical play 'Oliver' on Saturday, 28th February, 1988. The Head of the Drama department has asked you to carry out the following task:

Type an amended copy of the press release, in double or one and a half line spacing, which is to be sent to the local newspaper as part of the publicity campaign for the play.

(SEG; Specimen Paper)

PRESS RELEASE — (SP. CAPS.)

OLIVER!

¶ The pupils and ~~the~~ staff of the music and drama departments of the Broadwater middle school have been putting the final touches to their production of 'Oliver!' to be held at the school on Saturday 28 Feb 1988. The musical play, written by Lionel Bart, is based on Charles Dickens famous ~~late~~ story *u.c.* of Oliver Twist which pricked the consciences of Victorian England.

[BEADLE]

into employment

The story revolves around an orphan boy who is brought up in the local workhouse by the Beadle and then sold *£*. Unhappy, Oliver runs away, but falls into bad company when he meets the artful Dodger and is introduced by Fagin and his band of vagabond thieves.

accidents
stet. Several ~~misfortunes~~ befall Oliver before he is eventually united
· with his grandfather and the "rule of law" is re-established in the East End of London.

The musical involves more than 70 pupils and staff in the trs chorus, cast and orchestra. The performance is to be held in the Main School Hall beginning at 7·30pm and admission is by ticket which costs £1·50, available from the school office.

TASK 3

Prepare the list of new members under the headings – name, address, telephone number (3 separate columns in tabulated form). (LEAG; 1988)

VADS
List of members

Mr T B Filton, Eaves Lane, Denham, Norfolk, NR4 3ST Tel 0379-218
Miss J Harvey, Parsons Walk, Halesworth Norfolk, NR17 1QP
Tel 098-67-450
Mr G G Williams, Engelfield Green, Denham, Norfolk, NR4 3ST
Tel 0379-126 _ Barton
Mrs D ~~Moores~~, Ridgeway, Westbrook Road, Merfield, NR11 9ES
Tel 0676-1211
Mr T Sharples, 16 Swainsley Gardens, Castleton, Norfolk, NR13 2DP,
Tel 0231-161
Miss S H Baxter, 16 Wentworth Road, Castleton, Norfolk, NR13 2ET
Miss J Ford, 61 Castle Hill Road, Castleton, Norfolk, NR13 7JR
Miss C J James, 130 Calder Lane, Harleston, Norfolk, NR17 1QP.

Typist
Please list in alphabetical order of surname –
it will make it easier to add to our other
list later.

STUDENT ANSWERS TO COURSEWORK TASKS

TASK 1

66 Vertical alignment weak. 99

66 Make use of both lines. 99

66 This information was available from Task 1 of the set assignment. 99

66 Poor use of interliner. Too low. 99

66 Poor use of interliner. Too high. 99

66 Dashes omitted. 99

66 Inconsistent representation of date. Year missing. 99

Castleton Leisure Centre

The Croft
Castleton
Norfolk NR13 2CT

BOOKING FORM

I wish to book the following facilities in the Leisure Centre

NAME OF APPLICANT Chris Davies

HOME ADDRESS 222 Ash Hall Road, Castleton, Norfolk NR7 3SR

TELEPHONE NUMBER (home) _____ (business) 0231-6790

NAME OF SOCIETY Amateur Dramatic Society

MEETING FACILITIES

Large Hall (with stage)
Date(s) required 26 April 1988 to 30 April 1988

Large Meeting Hall
Date(s) required 25 February and 3 March 1988

Small Committee Room
(Date(s) required) _____

OTHER FACILITIES
Hire of Crockery: 36 cups   36 saucers
                      ___ small plates   50 large plates
                      ___ wine glasses   ___ tumblers

Date(s) required 26th April 1988
Special Lighting (give date(s) required) 27 to 30 April

I agree to pay for any damage or breakages.
Signed _____   Date 11 December 1987

Examiner Comments

You will notice that some information which the student has inserted, or should have inserted, was not given in the question. As previously explained, the fact that assignments are written around a theme means that such information will have been extracted from previous tasks. In this case, the address and telephone number (home) of the producer was gleaned from the headed paper supplied for another task.

This form presented a good opportunity for vertical alignment. If it is not possible to align *all* the information vertically, care should be taken to commence typing an equal distance from the printed information in each case.

TASK 2

PRESS RELEASE ✗   66 **Spaced capitals. No underscore.** 99

OLIVER ○

66 **Month in full.** 99

The pupils and staff of the Music and drama departments of the Broadwater

Middle School have been putting the final touches to their production of

'Oliver' to be held at the school on Saturday 28 Feb 1988. The musical

play, written by Lionel Bant, is based on Charles Dickens famous story of

Oliver Twist which pricked the consciences of Victorian Englans

66 **No need for capitals.** 99

The story revoles around an orphen boy who is brought up in the local

workhouse by the BEADLE and then sold into employment. Unhappy, Oliver

runs away, but falls into bad company ;when he meets the Artful Dodger a-

nd is introduced to Fagin and his band of vagabond theives.

66 **Incorrect line-end division.** 99

Several accidents befall Oliver before he is eventually limited with his

grandfather and the "rule of law" is re-established in the East End of Lon-

don.

66 **Incorrect line-end division.** 99

The musical involves more than 70 pupils and staff in the cast chorus, and

orchestra. The performance is to be held in the Main School Hall beginning

at 7.30 pm and admission is by ticket which costs £1.50, available from the

school office.

66 **Comma missing.** 99

Examiner   Comments

Although there are not many typing errors, this student has made some rather elementary 'theory' errors. Let us look at some of the points which have caused a loss of marks:

1   The heading should have been in spaced capitals and, as there was no line under it in the draft, it would have been advisable to omit the underscore.

     The exclamation mark has been omitted after Oliver. Perhaps this character did not appear on the student's typewriter. It could have been made by the use of an apostrophe and a fullstop.

2   The handwriting was not very clear at times but with a little more effort I am sure the student could have deduced that the 'd' in drama on the first line should have been a capital – after all the word 'music' had a capital letter.

     Perhaps the misreading of 'Bant' for 'Bart' in the first paragraph is understandable but the incorrect spelling of 'orphan' in the second paragraph is inexcusable since a dictionary could have been used to check.

     The mis-reading of the word 'united' in the third paragraph is also inexcusable. If the candidate had read through the passage it would have been obvious that 'limited' did not make sense in the sentence.

3   The incorrect spelling of 'thieves' (second paragraph) could have been a typing error

or it could have been that this candidate is not touch-typing but thought that this was the correct spelling!

TASK 3

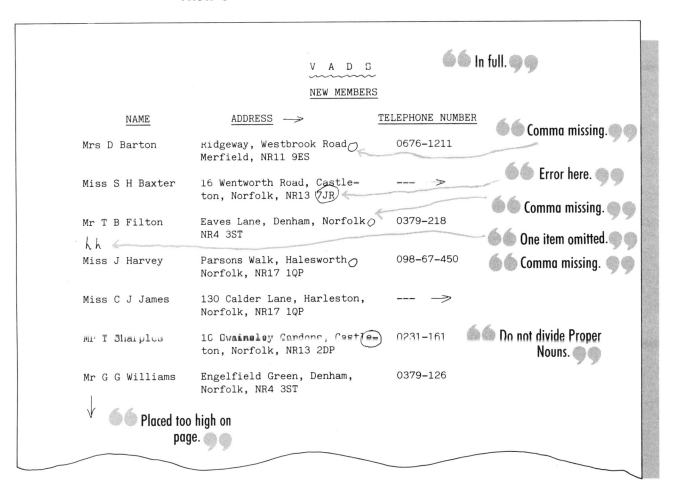

This is basically a well-displayed attempt, although the vertical placement is not quite accurate – just a little too high.

One quite important error is the omission of one of the items of information viz. details of Miss J. Ford.

The heading should have been typed in full. This particular Coursework Assignment was based on the theme of the work of the secretary to the **Villagers Amateur Dramatic Society**. The full name could have been extracted from the main instructions for the assignment or from previous tasks.

The student has chosen the standard layout for the tabulation but the word 'Address' over the second column is not quite in the centre. In fact all three columnar headings would have looked neater in initial capitals rather than block capitals.

Where there is no information to be inserted – as in the two instances in the last column – a single hyphen would have been sufficient. However, the use of three hyphens would not have been penalized had they been typed *centrally*, to conform to the standard layout.

USEFUL FOLLOW-UP WORK

SIMPLE COPYING   ### TASK 1

Type a copy of the following passage on A4 plain paper in double line spacing. Leave
margins of at least 25 mm (1 inch).

(SEG; 1988)

One of the most exciting places for a holiday in the USA is
Central Florida. Not only is it the home of Walt Disney
World it is also where the Space Shuttle blasts into orbit
from the Kennedy Space Centre. Other attractions include
Orlando Sea World and Busch Gardens, both of which add
their own magic to the area.

Clean sandy beaches, blue skies and a first class hotel
all help to complete the scene for a perfect holiday.

The Oceanside Inn Hotel, built specially for Elite Group
Holidays is situated on Cocoa Beach - the closest to Walt
Disney World - and is within easy driving distance of all
the main attractions.

TASK 2

Type a copy of the following passage on A4 plain paper in double line spacing. Leave
margins of at least 25 mm (1 inch).

(SEG; 1988)

Sport is probably the fastest growing leisure activity in
Britain today. Since the 'Sport for All' campaign of the
1970's, many thousands of people - both young and old -
have taken up a new sport.

But which sports do they play? Undoubtedly the most popular
new indoor activity is badminton, closely followed by squash
and swimming. Football, cricket, hockey and rugby continue
as the most popular outdoor sports

More money, the desire for better health and more leisure
time have all led to a growing demand for local sports
facilities.

TASK 3 (SEG; 1988)

Form Completion.

James Burnett of 46 Edward Road, Guildford, Surrey, GU6 5TX,
wishes to make a reservation for his family on holiday
number KHC 463 for 13 nights. The full party includes Mr
Burnett, his wife Christine and his two daughters, Katie
aged 12 and Lucy aged 8.

Mr Burnett intends to drive to Southampton to board the ship
there and will require parking facilities. He also requires
further details of insurance cover.

Please complete the necessary Holiday Reservation Form,
dated today, ready for signature.

ELITE GROUP HOLIDAY CRUISES

HOLIDAY RESERVATION

Full Name: _____

Address: _____

_____

_____ Postcode: _____

Holiday No: _____ Number of nights: _____

Please give details of all party members below

	Mr/Mrs Miss/Ms	Initials	Surname	Age if under 18
1				
2				
3				
4				
5				
6				

Do you require further details of
Elite Group Insurance?   YES/NO

Do you require car parking facilities?   YES/NO
If YES, please indicate which port   TILBURY/SOUTHAMPTON

_____   _____

(Signature)   *(Date)*

WORKING FROM MANUSCRIPT

TASK 4

Type a copy of the following on A4 plain paper. Leave a minimum top margin of 50 mm (2 inches) and a left margin of 37 mm (1½ inches).   (SEG; 1988)

> ,WIN FABULOUS PRIZES (spaced caps)
>
> ENTER OUR FREE COMPETITION
>
> Shopping from home using your Elite Group Mail Order Catalogue is full of fun and friendliness. From the moment you phone through on our 'fastfone' order line you begin to experience it.
>
> Inset 15 sp. ⎰ And to add to the fun we are giving you the opportunity to win some really fabulous prizes - cars, holidays, cash - in this free and exciting competition. trs
>
> ¶ of ⎱ How would you like to win a brand new Mini Metro? Or take an exotic holiday in the beautiful island paradise of Barbados? Or have the equivalent prize value in cash?
>
> Entering is simple. Just telephone through an order for any one of a selected range of women's clothes and your name will automatically be entered in our free draw to take place on 2 Jan 1989. It couldn't be easier!
>
> DON'T DELAY - TELEPHONE TODAY

TASK 5

Type a copy of the Constitution. Use A4 paper and blocked paragraphs.   (LEAG; 1989)

> caps St Paul's YC
>
> Constitution
>
> 1. The organisation will be known as
> caps St Paul's youth club.
> (no underscore)
>
> 2. Being attached to St Paul's church, the address for correspondence will be c/o St Paul's Vicarage, Elm Road, Woodley, Reading. RG4 9UY.
>
> ¶ 3. The club will be operate be open on Tuesday + Thurs. evenings 7-10pm, in the church Hall attached to St Paul's church. (meeting)
>
> will be
> 4. Membership is Open to young people between the ages of 13 + 25 yrs - Christians or non-Christians.

5. A joining fee of 50p will be charged. Attendance at each meeting

Stet ~~will~~ cost ~~10p~~ 20p.

6. Members will be allowed to bring along 1 non-member guest to any meeting. Members will, at all times, be held responsible for the good behaviour of their guests.

7. An annual gen. meeting, at which all paid up members will be entitled to vote, will be held in January of each year.

8. The object of the club will be to provide recreational facilities + a meeting place for young people of all faiths. Events of special interest will be organised at intervals throughout the year.

9. The Group Leader + Secretary will be responsible for running the club and Rev Thomas O'Malley, Vicar of St Paul's, will be an ex officio member of all committees.

10. Besides the (AGM) ⌐in full!, ad hoc committees may be formed to organise special events or deal with pressing administrative matters. One-third of those eligible to attend such meetings will be required to produce a quorum.

N.B.

Please make item 8 the 4th item, renumbering the rest of the items as necessary.

DISPLAY **TASK 6**

Display the following attractively on A5 paper.

Caps + u/s   WOODTHORPE PLAYERS
present
REBECCA

Sp. Caps

a play in three acts
by
Daphne du Maurier
Thursday, Friday and Saturday
23, 24, 25 March in
Community Arts Theatre
Springfield Road
Woodthorpe
at 8 pm
Tickets – £5, £3, and £2.50
Obtainable from the Theatre box office
Telephone 0933 568748

TASK 7

Using A5 paper, display the following advertisement. Pay particular attention to horizontal and vertical placement.

PAM'S PANTRY
High St
Cirencester
Glos

Friendly restaurant situated in the centre of ~~the~~ *this* beautiful
u/c Cotswold town,

Caps +   { Luncheons
centre   { Afternoon Teas
each   { Dinners
line

OPEN   Tuesdays to Saturdays inclusive
12 noon ~~till~~ 12 midnight

Caps
no u/s   Excellent cuisine   Fully licensed

TABULATION

TASK 8

Type a copy of the following on suitable paper, centring the table vertically and horizontally.   (SEG; 1988)

ELITE GROUP HOLIDAY CRUISE TARIFFS

CABIN CODE	AVAILABLE CABINS	12 NIGHTS £	6/7 NIGHTS £	12/13 NIGHTS £
A1	Deluxe Suites			
	Separate Lounge, bath	2412	1395	2650
A2	Deluxe Suites			
	twin beds, lounge, bath	2275	1355	2500
B1	Outside Twin Cabins			
	double bed, lounge, shower	1983	1026	1995
B2	Outside Twin Cabins[1]			
	twin beds, veranda, bath	2065	1100	2105
C1	Inside Twin Cabins			
	double bed, shower	1640	895	1710
C2	Inside Twin Cabins			
	double bed, shower	1640	895	1710
C2/T	Inside Twin Cabins			
	twin beds, bath	1625	854	1695
D1	Single Inside Cabins[2]			
	with bath or shower	1054	695	1100

All cabins are equipped w a multi-channel music system,
colour television, refrigerator and telephone.

1. Only avail on the starboard side of the vessel.
2. A limited number of these cabins can accommodate a second
   person sharing at a supplement of £300.

TASK 9

Display the following table on A4 plain paper. Centre vertically and horizontally.

AMERICAN FREEDOM

FLY/DRIVE RATES FOR ~~1987/88~~ 1988/89

please keep the abbreviations in the headings

COLLECTION POINT	1 AUG TO 31 OCT	1 NOV TO 30 APRTL	1 MAY TO 7 JUNE	8 JUNE TO 31 JULY
New York	439	369	419	439
Chicago	409	319	379	409
Boston	479	399	(376)	469 *hrs.*
San Francisco	406	316	(449)	406
⁊ Detroit	~~406~~	~~340~~	~~376~~	~~406~~
Washington	559	449	540	570
Los Angeles	580	470	540	570
Cape Canaveral	439	369	419	439

All prices are in £ Sterling and are based on 4 persons sharing one car.

For any party of less than 4 persons a supplement of £35 will be added to the above prices

please leave 2 clear line spaces here

REARRANGEMENT OF INFORMATION

TASK 10

Type the following table on A4 paper.

Prestige Homes PLC
Estate Agents

HOUSES FOR SALE
in West Bickington

Column 2 before Column 1 please

Detached or Semi-Detached	Address of property	No. of Bedrooms	Price £
D	46 Nightingale Rd	3	95,000
D	17 Ferndale Avenue	3	90,500
D	Pear Tree Cottage Elm Lane	4	115,000
D	Bramble Lodge, The Planks	5	126,000
D	91 Turnpike Road	3	96,950
S/D	106 Huntingdon Avenue	3	81,500
S/D	14 Moors Place	2	77,950
S/D	82 Birdlip Hill	3	90,950
S/D	41 Chessington Crescent	2	72,500
D	St. Judes, Rosemary Court	4	106,000

Typist!
please rearrange in price order starting with the highest price.

LAYOUT OF BUSINESS DOCUMENTS

BUSINESS LETTERS

OTHER TYPES OF LETTER

ENVELOPES

MEMORANDA

CARBON COPIES

TELEPHONE MESSAGES

POSTCARDS

GETTING STARTED

A large proportion of office typing and word processing involves letters and memoranda for which there are a number of accepted types of **layout**. The over-riding necessity, in the office situation, is to follow the 'Rule of the House'; that is, the accepted practice used throughout the firm. However, in this chapter we shall look at the main forms of layout to which you will be expected to adhere in the examination. Once again, the most important principle is *consistency*.

Chapter 6 deals with the **composition** of these forms of communication which is another area tested in GCSE. Whether you are copying from typescript or manuscript or composing your own correspondence, it is important to observe the generally accepted rules of display.

E S S E N T I A L   P R I N C I P L E S

1 ❯ BUSINESS LETTERS

SIZE OF PAPER

Business letters are typed on the firm's headed paper. On both A4 and A5 paper the printed heading is placed at the top of the *shorter* edge; in other words the paper is used **portrait**. The printed heading includes the name of the firm, the address and telephone number. Other information may include, telex number, type of business, firm's logo, details of other branches or names of directors. There may be a space allocated for 'Our ref' or 'Your ref'. If this is the case, be sure to place the references at this point.

CHOICE OF PAPER

> ❝ Short letters look better in single line spacing with wide margins, than spread over the whole sheet. ❞

In most cases you will be issued with A4 and A5 headed paper. You will need to choose which to use. Remember you must leave a minimum left hand margin of 1″ (25 mm) on A4 paper and ½″ (13 mm) on A5. Letters are seldom typed in double line spacing but if you do choose to do so, remember that the name and address of addressee must *always* be typed in single line spacing.

    Vertical placement is also important so do not be tempted to start typing immediately after the printed heading. You should turn up *at least three lines* before commencing even the reference. If it is a short letter you can, of course, leave more space.

STYLES OF LAYOUT

There are three main methods of setting out a business letter. They are:

Fully blocked	Blocked	Semi-blocked

The most common form, and the one which is easiest and quickest to use in an examination, is the fully-blocked. In fact, some of the GCSE examination questions may *instruct* you to use this method.

SPACING BETWEEN PARTS OF A LETTER

The *usual* practice is to leave 2 clear line spaces (turn up 3) between the reference and date, the date and name and address of addressee, and between the end of the address and the salutation. Thereafter leave one clear space (turn up 2) between the parts of the letter or between paragraphs.

PARTS OF A LETTER NEEDING SPECIAL ATTENTION

Reference

This is made up of the initials of the dictator, followed by the initials of the typist. It may also include file numbers. You are often required to complete a reference by adding your own initials, for example JHT/(your initials)

Date

This is a most important part of the letter. In the examination you may be given an initial instruction to 'date all correspondence with today's date, unless otherwise instructed'. In subsequent drafts, letters or memos will not necessarily be dated but you must be sure to include the date.

There are several accepted methods of indicating the date. Here are the most common:

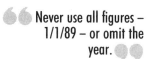

Never use all figures – 1/1/89 – or omit the year.

1st January, 1989	January 1st, 1989
1 January 1989	January 1 1989

Signature block

Your letter may simply end with the complimentary close (e.g. Yours faithfully), or you may also be required to type the name of the firm and the name and designation of the person signing the letter. For example:

Yours faithfully
MINEHEAD PRODUCTS LTD

J H Turner
Sales Manager

Notice there is no space between the 'Yours faithfully' and the name of the firm but sufficient space (approximately 5 clear lines) must be left for the signature.

Enclosures

There are several methods of indicating that other documents accompany the letter. The most common is to type 'Enc' or 'Enc (2)' at the foot of the letter – approximately five line spaces from the end of the signature block and against the left margin. However, some firms choose to indicate enclosures by putting a mark (possibly an asterisk, an oblique sign or three dots) in the left margin against the line of the text which mentions the enclosures. When typing a letter watch out for the reference to enclosures and be sure to indicate this in some way. This is often a part of the 'test' and the abbreviation 'Enc' will not necessarily be shown in the draft, or the instructions.

EXTRA PARTS OF A LETTER

The following may be used in some letters:
- **CONFIDENTIAL** This is usually typed a clear line space above the name and address of the addressee.
- **RECORDED DELIVERY** As for Confidential.
- **For the attention of Mr P Bassett** This is typed one clear line space below the name and address of addressee. On an envelope it is typed above the name and address so if the letter is likely to be sent in a window envelope the attention line should be typed a clear line space above this name and address.
- **Subject heading** This merely states what the letter is about. It is placed one clear line space after the salutation. In the semi-blocked layout it is centred on the writing line. It may be typed with initial capitals and underscored or block capitals without underscore.

OPEN AND CLOSED (STANDARD) PUNCTUATION

In personal letter-writing you have probably been used to inserting punctuation at the ends of the lines of the address and indicating abbreviations by the use of a full stop. For example:

Mr A. B. Castle,
26 Fordbridge Road,
Swindon.
SN2 4BZ

This is known as **closed** or standard punctuation. When this form is used it is also necessary to insert the comma in the date and to include a comma after the salutation (Dear Sir,) and after the complimentary close (Yours faithfully,).

However, the modern trend is to omit all these punctuation points so that an address would look like this:

Mr A B Castle		Mr AB Castle
26 Fordbridge Road	**or**	26 Fordbridge Road
SWINDON		SWINDON
SB2 4BZ		SB2 4BZ

It is important not to confuse the two.

As it is usual to use **open** punctuation with fully-blocked layout, you would be wise to forget about the commas and full stops in addresses and abbreviations.

Do remember that **consistency** is all-important. When using open punctuation it would be incorrect to refer (in the letter) to, say, 'your appointment for 2 p.m.' The time must be written as 2 pm – no full stop to denote the abbreviation.

It is also advisable to type the date as 1 January 1989 rather than 1st January 1989. Again, be careful not to refer in the letter to 'your letter of the 30**th** December' when you have used the style omitting the 'th' at the top of the letter.

Courtesy titles is another area where you might easily confuse open and closed punctuation. Note the following:

Open punctuation	*Closed punctuation*
J R Standish Esq BA	J. R. Standish, Esq., B. A.,
Messrs Brown & Green	Messrs. Brown & Green,
Rev T S Crochett	Rev. T. S. Crochett,
Meredith Saxon & Co Ltd	Meredith, Saxon & Co. Ltd.,

Let's pause and look at the beginning of a letter typed by a candidate:

```
Ref  ST/yr initials

    Date!!

Unique Bathrooms Ltd.

27 The Centre

STAINES

TW18 3TS

Dear Sirs,

Order No 4693

I refer to my order of the 22nd January which you assured me

would receive your urgent attention .........
```

As you can see, the candidate has already made a number of mistakes all of which will be penalized. The reference should have been completed with the candidate's initials – the instruction should not have been typed!

The full stop after Ltd and the comma after the salutation means that there is confusion between open and closed punctuation and, of course, there should never be a full stop after headings and underscoring should not extend beyond the last letter.

And what about the date? **All** correspondence should be dated.

CONTINUATION SHEETS

Occasionally a letter is very long and will not fit on to one sheet. If a second sheet is needed use plain bond paper (not headed). Head the second sheet with the number of the page, the name of the addressee and the date. Notice the different layouts to match the general form adopted:

Fully-blocked

> 2
> Feltham Plastics Ltd
> 25 June 1988

Blocked or semi-blocked

Feltham Plastics Ltd   2   25TH June 1988

Always leave a space of at least 1″ (6 lines) at the foot of the first page and at the top of the second page.

Now turn to the end of this chapter and study the questions on this topic.

---

2 ⟩ OTHER TYPES OF LETTER

CIRCULAR LETTERS

These are business letters which contain the same information but are sent to different customers. It is common practice to type the original letter on a stencil and have it duplicated. Space may be left for later inclusion of the name and address of addressee. If it is not felt necessary to include this information it is usual to leave 3 clear spaces after the date before the salutation.

The *salutation* may consist of the word 'Dear' only – the remainder being typed in at a later stage, or it may be given as 'Dear Sir/Madam'.

The *date* may be given as the month and year only or the words 'Date as postmark' may be typed in place of the date.

Circular letters are now more likely to be produced on a word processor, which can store the standard letter and merge it with a list of names and addresses. This gives a more individual touch to the letter.

STANDARD (FORM) LETTERS

Where letters of a similar nature are frequently sent out it may be prudent to prepare a *form letter* with spaces into which individual information can be inserted.

This is a good test in an examination and can be treated similarly to a task of form filling. An example of such a question is given at the end of this chapter.

PERSONAL LETTERS

You may be asked to write a *personal* letter in your GCSE examination, particularly in the section which is testing your ability to compose a letter.

As this letter is coming from an individual, headed paper will not be used. In the examination, select a piece of plain bond paper (A4 or A5 portrait) and type your own address at the top right-hand side, in alignment with the right-hand margin. If you use the fully-blocked style of layout it is permissible to type your own address against the left margin.

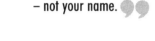 Type your address only – not your name.

Ensure that your *signature* is clear or type your name (and courtesy title) after the signature.

---

3 ⟩ ENVELOPES

You will almost certainly be required to type at least one **envelope**. You will probably be provided with an envelope either the C6 size, which measures 6⅜″ × 4½″ (162 × 114 mm) and is used to take A4 paper folded twice or A5 paper folded once, or the DL size 8⅝″ × 4¼″ (220 × 110 mm) which takes A4 paper folded in three. If an envelope is not provided you will be asked to rule a rectangle or fold a piece of paper to represent an envelope. A5 paper folded in half is roughly the same size as a C6 envelope and A4 folded in three can be used to represent the larger envelope.

There are various methods of setting out the address but the following rules should be observed:

1   The address should occupy the lower half of the envelope – begin typing at the half-way point measured vertically.
2   Begin approximately 50mm in from the left side or centralize the longest line.

3   Use the fully-blocked style of layout and single-line spacing. On envelopes, double-line spacing may be more easily read.
4   Always type the town in block capitals.
5   Type the post code on a separate line or at least six clear spaces from other information contained on the line. There should be no full stop after the post code.
6   Take care to use the correct courtesy title. No courtesy title is required when writing to a limited company.
7   'For the attention of . . .' should be typed one clear line space above the address.
8   Private, Confidential etc. may be typed above and to the left of the address.

Examples of setting out addresses are as follows:

Block style – open punctuation

Messrs Brightwell & Co
Lyon House
Mortimer Street
London   EP4 4PF

or

For the attention of Mr J R Barrett

The Tinplate Production Co Ltd
Foundry Works
Greenfield Trading Estate
WIDNES
WA3 4TD

4 > MEMORANDA

> **Notice this is opposite to short letters, which are typed on A5 portrait paper.**

A memorandum (often called a *memo*) is a form of internal communication between branches or departments of the same firm. It is less formal than the letter and, as it is used within the firm it differs somewhat in layout.

There is no salutation or complimentary close. Headings, which are usually printed, indicate to whom the memo is addressed and who sent it. Like the letter is may have a reference and a subject heading, and, of course, it must always be *dated*.

Memos are often short and so can be typed on A5 paper. The paper is *usually* used landscape. Longer memos are typed on A4 paper and may even require a continuation sheet.

There are various methods of setting out the information at the beginning of a memo. Obviously, when a form is provided you need to put the information in the correct positions for that particular form.

Here are a few alternatives.

MEMORANDUM

TO   Sales Manager

FROM   Managing Director   Date: 1st June 1989

MEMORANDUM

TO   Mr J Brown   Date: 1st June 1989

FROM   T Short   Ref: JB/ML

MEMORANDUM

TO   Supervisor, Mailroom   FROM   Personnel Officer

                                                                          1st June 1989

```
MEMORANDUM

TO          Supervisor, Mailroom

FROM        Personnel Officer

DATE        1st June 1989

SUBJECT     Replacement junior clerk
```

Where a form is *printed* it may contain dotted lines on which to insert the information. There may be a continuous line below the information to set the printed headings apart from the message.

The last style above is the fully-blocked method and would be used with blocked paragraphs. In all other styles, blocked or indented paragraphs may be used and the subject heading (if any) can be centralized over the body of the work or typed against the left margin if blocked paragraphs are used.

Notice that these headings and the information they contain are displayed in double line spacing.

When inserting information against items 'To', 'From', 'Date' etc., be sure to align vertically as in the suggestions above or type the information an equal distance from the printed word. For example:

TO   Mr J Smith

FROM   Mr J Brown

Now look at the specimen question at the end of this chapter.

5 > **CARBON COPIES**

It is usually important to take a **carbon copy** of all outgoing letters or memos. You can, therefore, expect this element to be tested in an examination. Remember that the copies are taken on plain flimsy paper, rather than headed paper.

You will need to practise inserting sheets of paper with carbon paper between, ensuring that the shiny (inked) side of the carbon paper goes against the paper on which you want the copy to appear. *Handle carbon paper with care.* It is surprising how much of the ink gets on to your fingers and is then transferred to other work. If handled too much, you might find the copy of the letter has many ugly smudges on it.

Quite often you are requested to take more than one copy, since other people will be receiving copies of the letter or memo. In this case it is usual to type 'cc' – followed by the name(s) of people receiving copies – at the foot of the letter or at the top or bottom of the memo:

cc Mr Brown
     Ms Jones
     Mrs Summers

You may also be required to type the name of the person at the top left or right side of the copy. Another method of 'routing' (directing) the copies to specific people is to underline *one* of the names on *each* of the carbon copies.

CORRECTING CARBON COPIES

> ❝ Do not forget to remove the scrap paper before typing in the correction. ❞

Whilst most electronic machines have a self-correcting device, this is of little use when there is a carbon copy. This is because, in order to correct an error, the letter is 'struck over', thus resulting in an overtype on the carbon copy.

To make a correction when there is a carbon copy, treat the *back* copy first, by erasing the error with liquid Tippex or by the use of a typing rubber. Next, place a piece of scrap paper between the carbon paper and the copy and correct the top copy. Remove the scrap paper and retype with the correct letter.

Uncorrected, or badly corrected, carbon copies will be penalized in an examination.

6 > **TELEPHONE MESSAGES**

In most offices you will find a pad of **telephone message** forms near each telephone. When a call is taken for an absent colleague it is essential that full details of the message are recorded and left for the colleague to attend to on his or her return.

A large part of the typing of telephone messages is obviously a case of form filling – putting information into relevant sections. The following are examples of different types of telephone message forms:

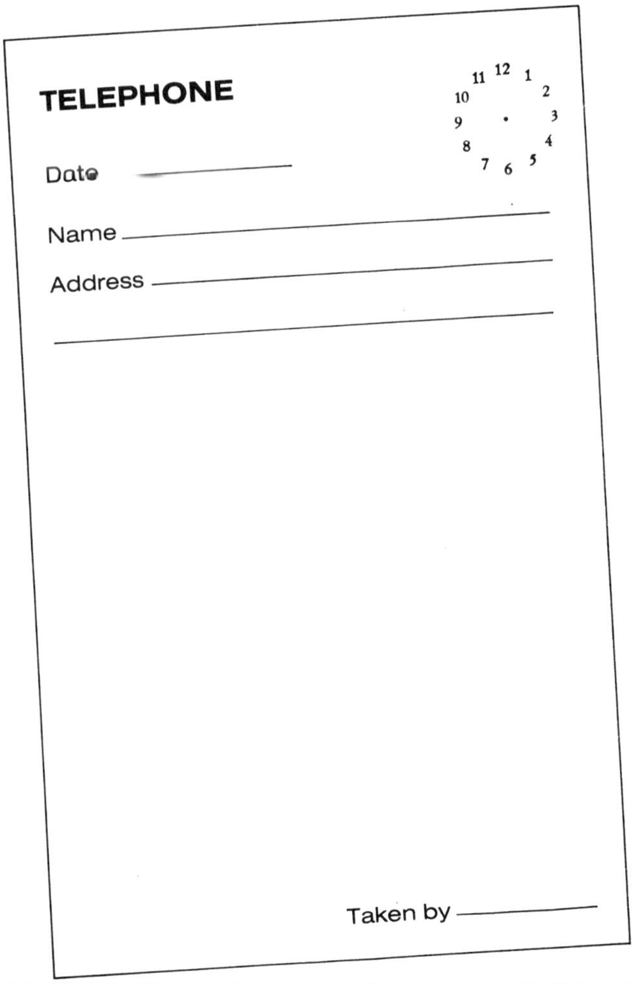

TELEPHONE

11 12 1
10 · 2
9 3
8 4
7 6 5

Date _____

Name _____

Address _____

_____

Taken by _____

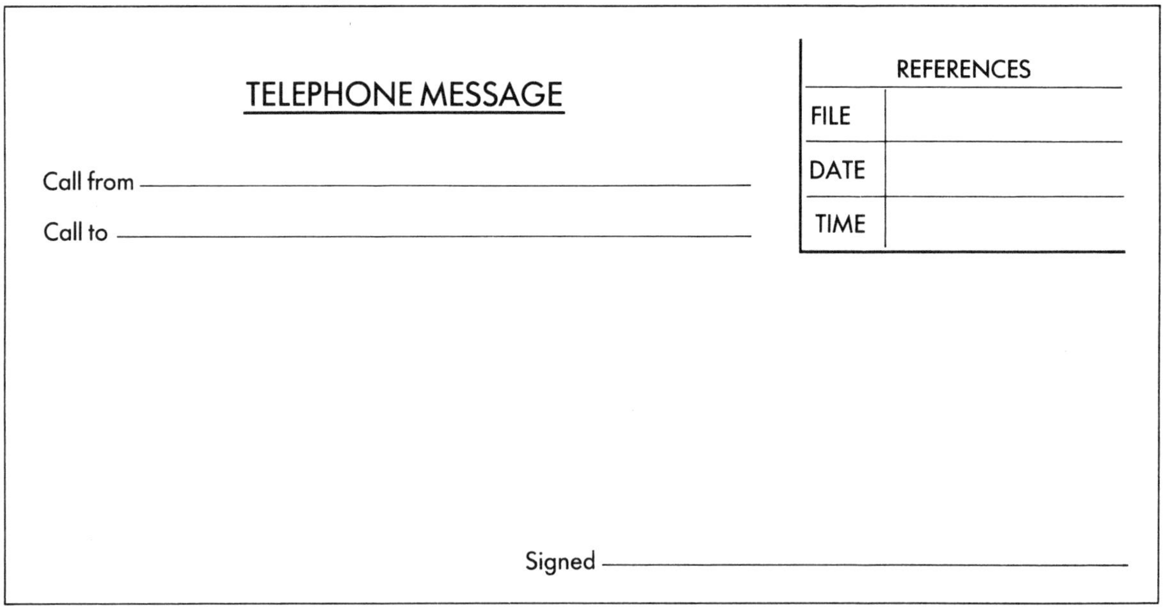

TELEPHONE MESSAGE

Call from _____

Call to _____

	REFERENCES
FILE	
DATE	
TIME	

Signed _____

Apart from essential information such as who the message is *for*, who it was *from* and *when* the call was taken, there is the message itself. In the GCSE examination you may be given a telephone message from which you are then asked to compose a letter or memo. You may be given a set of facts, or a record of a conversation, and requested to compose the message. If this is the case be sure to use *reported* speech. The most common type of question will be an exercise which merely asks you to type a message on to the special form.

In either case, pay attention to *display*. Use suitable margins to ensure that the message is not cramped and be consistent in the paragraph style used. Make sure you *sign* the form (unless instructed otherwise). This usually means a signature, not a typed name.

An exercise of this nature is given at the end of this chapter.

7 ▷ POSTCARDS

Some firms use **postcards** to acknowledge receipt of correspondence or orders or to confirm appointments. Usually the card has the firm's heading printed at the top, but if this is not the case it is left to the typist to display the name and address of the firm from which the card is being sent.

Be sure not to type too close to the top edge. Leave at least 3 clear spaces before beginning the name. Narrow margins on the right and left (approximately ½″) are quite adequate.

The message is kept *brief*, usually with no salutation or complimentary close. The date might simply be 'as postmark'.

On the *reverse side* is typed the name and address of the addressee – using the same rules as apply to envelop addressing.

Cards of roughly A6 size are also used for typing such documents as itineraries, so it is important to gain some practice in typing within this restricted space and on to card. When using some typewriters you may have difficulty getting the card to bend round the platen. Make sure that the paper fingers are placed well over the card to help the grip and never type right to the bottom edge.

EXAMINATION QUESTIONS

Let us look at some examples of questions which have been set on these areas of the syllabuses.

BUSINESS LETTERS   Question 1

> Typist: carbon copy and envelope, please
>
> Our ref TMW/RVS
>
> Mrs J Stephens
> 27 Bligh Road
> Gravesend
> Kent
> DA19 1NQ
>
> Dear Mrs S—
>
> I ack. receipt of yr. letter of 10 March regarding the showers at the Praxi Leisure Centre, and am sorry to hear of the problems you have recently encountered.

Difficulties in supplying hot water to the showers during periods of peak usage have been experienced for some ~~considerable~~ time.

The indications are that when you take your shower, ie at approx. 8.00pm on a Friday, many other participants in various activities are also using the shower facilities; this naturally puts a strain on the system, resulting in the hot water tanks being drained faster than the boilers can cope with demand.

This matter is of great concern to the centre management, and I can assure you that positive steps are now being taken to investigate ways of ensuring a ~~permanent~~ constant supply of hot water to all changing-rooms.

I wl. make myself available on a Fri. evening if you wish to discuss the matter further, but in the meantime I hope you will continue to use the facilities of the centre. (and enjoy)

Yours sincerely

TM WILLIAMSON
Praxi Leisure Centre PLC

(RSA)

Question 2

Background information

You have offered to help the Secretary of the Off-Beats Fan Club with some typing in preparation for the group's forthcoming UK tour. The Off-Beats is a Country and Western Singing group from the USA.

The name of the Secretary is   Miss Diane Holmes

You will need the following addresses

The Royal Hotel
Bayswater Road
London
W2 4RJ

Mr Abdul Khan
43 Bridge Street
Liverpool
Merseyside
L56 2EF

Telephone number   051-525 3678

Use today's date and the Secretary's initials/your initials as a reference wherever appropriate.

Task

Type the following letter to Mr Abdul Khan using the A4 letterhead provided. Take a carbon copy and type an envelope. Correct any spelling errors.

Dr. Mr Khan

Thankyou for your cheque and completed aplication form.

I am pleased to welcome you as a member of the Off-Beats Fan Club and hope you will be able to take advantage of the many privileges this gives you.

1 You will receive a quaterly newsletter giving up-to-date news of the group's activities as well as advance notice of new releases, concert dates and proposed tours.

2 Regular meetings are organised for fan club members +, in order to minimise travelling expenses, these are arranged on an area basis.

3 New members will be sent a signed photograph of the group members of their choice. I note that you have requested a photograph of the piano player and you should receive this within a few days.

I wish you many happy hours of listening to the off-Beats.

Yours Scly.

(insert name)
Fan club secretary

You will be informed of the date, time and place of these meetings by your regional secretary.

ADVICE AND COMMENTS: BUSINESS LETTERS

Question 1

The instructions are kept to a minimum, so you will need to use your discretion to a certain extent. You will almost certainly have been provided with headed paper both A4 and A5 so you should choose the headed A4.

You need to take a carbon copy. Select a piece of plain flimsy paper for this.

Remember the *date*. No date has been given on the letter but there was an instruction on the front of the question paper which stated: 'Insert today's date on letters and memos, unless otherwise instructed'. So, do not forget.

Notice that the salutation is incomplete. You need to type: Dear Mrs Stephens.

There are *three* corrections to be made for which you might have expected marginal correction signs: *viz.* the transposition in the first paragraph, the fact that the second and third paragraphs run on to each other and that a new paragraph has to be started after 'demand'.

There are also two other corrections, one an alteration at the end of the penultimate (last but one) paragraph and the other an insertion to be made in the last paragraph.

There is a slight difference from standard practice in the signature block. Notice that the name of the firm is typed under the signature rather than directly after the complimentary close. If in doubt it is always a good idea to follow the layout as indicated in the draft, so in this case type the name of the firm *below* the signature.

This letter is in good, clear handwriting and is clearly set out in the fully-blocked style with open punctuation, so you should find it a relatively simple test.

Question 2

Although this is clearly written, there are a number of spelling mistakes you must look out for. There are also a number of hyphenated words, so remember how to deal with these. You have to research some information previously given and to insert the corrections indicated.

MEMORANDA

Question 3

On a suitable form, type the following memorandum from the Secretary of MEG Enterprises Vegetarian Society (Mrs. Pauline Bradshaw) to Miss Sara Kaur, who is Secretary of MEG Enterprises Social Club. Correct the two spelling errors and the punctuation error, as well as making any other corrections indicated. Use blocked paragraphs and single line spacing.   (MEG; 1988)

Ref PB/ (your initials)

Today's date

As you probably know, we are hoping to organise a visit for our members' to a weekend wholefood conference in July. We have now recieved further details, including a specimen menu, which I am sending with this memo.

WHET

In order to whet our members' appetites, therefore, I should be greatful if you would display this on the notice-board in the social club, next to the Poster lc advertising the conference.

TYPIST Insert a subject heading WEEKEND WHOLEFOOD CONFERENCE

Question 4

Task

Type the following Memorandum from the Secretary to the Producer using the printed form provided.   (NEA; 1988)

¶   The auditions for parts for our autumn production of Bernard Shaw's 'Candida' have been arranged for wednesday, 13 July

stet   As you will see below there are only 6 ~~characters~~ *actors* in the cast. The costumes required are ordinary day clothes for the 4 men and 2 women involved.

lc   The Play will be performed for 6 evenings from Monday, 7 November, to Saturday, 12 November, at the Northern Theatre, Northchester, commencing at 7·30 pm.

←——————— 4 clear line spaces

Typist: Please keep dashes in line

CHARACTERS (in order of appearance)

[PROSERPINE]

Reverend James Morrell – clergy man
Miss Proserpine Gamett typist
Reverend Alexander Mill – young gentleman
Mr Burgess – man aged about 60
trs   Candida – [Pretty woman] well built ⌐
Eugene – shy youth

ADVICE AND COMMENTS

Question 3

Notice that you have to use the memo form supplied for this task. The memo is addressed:

TO   Miss Sara Kaur, Secretary of Social Club

FROM   Mrs. Pauline Bradshaw, Secretary of Vegetarian Society.

The handwriting is very clear and the writer has even taken the trouble to print clearly the word WHET since it is a word with which you might not be familiar.

You will need to take care with the apostrophe *s* – notice it comes after the s in members' because there is more than one member.

There is also a confusion of paragraphs in the draft. The first paragraph is in blocked form and the second in indented form. The instructions requested blocked paragraphs throughout.

Notice that the reference has to be completed with your initials.

Did you spot the two spelling errors – they were 'received' (first paragraph) and 'grateful' (second paragraph).

Notice that a subject heading is required. This should be typed at the beginning of the work – after the date but before the first paragraph. As it is shown in the draft as block capitals, it would be best to type this heading in block capitals without underscore rather than initial capitals with an underscore.

Question 4

In this case you are not required to make a choice in the size of paper used since the Group provided only A4 paper. It is important, therefore, to use wide margins and to leave some space after the heading in order to ensure that the work appears centrally on the page.

As the printed heading is given in blocked style, it is a good idea to retain this style throughout.

The memo contains quite a few numbers – '4 men and 2 women' and '6 evenings'. It is important to be consistent in the representation of these, not using '4 men and 2 women' followed by 'six evenings'. Either words or figures will be acceptable, so long as there is *consistency* throughout.

There is a date in the third paragraph. It is important to keep to the same format as used in the printed heading.

When required to 'leave 4 clear lines', it is important to turn up **5 lines** since you must allow for the line you are about to type on.

It is not necessary to plan the list of characters as a tabulated piece. All that is required is to count the letters and spaces in the longest name and ensure sufficient space is left before inserting the hyphen in the first character.

The handwriting is clear with few correction signs, although care has to be taken to retain the correct word (characters) in the second paragraph.

TELEPHONE MESSAGE

Question 5

At 1300 hours today Mrs Jean Brown of 46 Highbury Crescent, Liverpool L26 0BJ (telephone 051-469 6243) telephoned. She wanted to speak to the General Sales Manager, Mr. Peter Saunders, but he was out and you took the message.

Type the information on the telephone message form provided. Remember to sign the form. The message you took was:

Mrs. Brown's husband has died suddenly and she wants to know who to contact regarding his life assurance policy.

Would you please telephone her this afternoon or first thing tomorrow.

(LEAG; 1988)

STUDENT'S ANSWERS TO QUESTIONS 2 AND 5 WITH EXAMINER COMMENTS

BUSINESS LETTERS   Question 2

THE OFF-BEATS

Fan Club   Bloomsbury Street
London
WC1B 3QD

12th May 1988   Tel: 01-636 5610

Mr Abdul Khan
43 Bridge Street
LIVERPOOL
Merseyside
L56 2EF

In full!

No fullstop after numbers in open punctuation.

No spaces in a hyphenated word

Dr. Mr Khan

Thank you for your cheque and completed application form.

I am pleased to welcome you as a member of the Off - Beats Fan Club and hope you will be able to take advantage of the man privileges this gives you.

1. You will receive a quarterly newsletter giving up-to-date news of the group's activities as well as advance notice of new releases concert dates and proposed tours.

2. Regular meetings are organised for fan club members and, in order to minimise travelling expenses, these are arranged on area basis. You will be informed of the date, time and place of these meetings by your regional secretary.

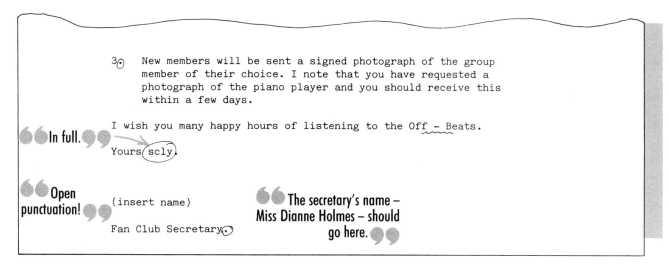

3. New members will be sent a signed photograph of the group member of their choice. I note that you have requested a photograph of the piano player and you should receive this within a few days.

I wish you many happy hours of listening to the Off - Beats.

Yours scly.

In full.

Open punctuation!

(insert name)

Fan Club Secretary.

The secretary's name – Miss Dianne Holmes – should go here.

The student has placed the letter nicely on the correct paper, although there are two instances where the right-hand margin has become ragged.

It is a pity there are some *uncorrected* typing errors. There has been some confusion between standard and open punctuation. When open punctuation is used there is no need to put a full stop after numbers and certainly there should be no full stop after 'Fan Club Secretary'. There is a great temptation to finish any exercise with a full stop, so this is quite a common mistake.

This student should have known that the words in the salutation and complimentary close should have been typed in full and that he/she was expected to look up the name of the Secretary in order to complete the signature block. After all, this student took the trouble to look up the name and address of addressee and correctly insert it.

TELEPHONE MESSAGE

Question 5

TELEPHONE MESSAGE

for Mr Peter Saunders   Dept General Sales Manager

Time 1300 hours   Name of Caller Mrs Jean Brown

Firm/Address 46 Highbury Crescent Liverpool L26 OBJ

Phone No 051 469 6243   Extn

Mrs Brown's husband has died suddenly and she wants

to know who to contact regarding his life assurance

policy.

Would you please telephone her this afternoon or

first thing tomorrow.

Date 16 May 1988   Message taken by   J. Bingley

On the face of it this seems a good attempt. Most of the information is in the correct place, apart from the fact that Mr Saunders' department is 'Sales' (the candidate has given his *position* rather than his department), and the candidate has correctly signed the form.

But now look at the actual typing. What a pity the candidate did not set the machine in double line spacing for the message. Had he/she done so there would not have been missed space after the second line.

Now study the use of the interliner. This is not very good, is it? Very few items are just 1 mm above the dotted line. In fact the form seems to have been inserted into the machine crooked, since some lines *slope* so that by the end of the line the words are touching the dots.

Remember that the information should be aligned vertically or typed an equal distance from the printed word. It is not possible to line the information vertically in this instance, but the candidate could have started typing, say, two spaces from the printed word or above, say, the fourth dot of the line in each case.

A TUTOR'S ANSWER TO QUESTION 4

MEMORANDA   Question 4

MEMORANDUM

To   Producer

From   Secretary

Date   11 May 1988

Ref   The auditions for parts for our autumn production of Bernard

        Shaw's 'Candida' have been arranged for Wednesday 13 July.

        As you will see below there are only 6 actors in the cast. The

        costumes required are ordinary day clothes for the 4 men and 2

        women involved.

        The play will be performed for 6 evenings from Monday,

        7 November, to Saturday 12 November, at the Northern Theatre,

        Northchester, commencing at 7.30 pm.

        CHARACTERS (in order of appearance)

        Reverend James Morrell   -   clergyman

        Miss Proserpine Garnett   -   typist

        Reverend Alexander Mill   -   young gentleman

        Mr Burgess   -   man aged about 60

        Candida   -   well-built pretty woman

        Eugene   -   shy youth

COURSEWORK ASSIGNMENT

TASK 1

Miss Harvey (see Chapter 4, Coursework Assignments, Task 3) was unable to attend the Committee Meeting. Complete the form letter to tell her the name of the next production – The Wind in the Willows. The first rehearsal is on 7 January 1988 beginning at 7.30 p.m. Type an envelope.

(LEAG; 1988)

```
              VILLAGERS AMATEUR DRAMATIC SOCIETY

     Please send correspondence to:            The Producer
                                               Chris Davies
                                               222 Ash Hall Road
                                               Castleton
                                               Norfolk  NR7 2SR

     Date as Postmark                          Tel: 0231-55780




     Dear

     It was decided at our last meeting that the next performance

     will be                          and I enclose a script

     for you to look at.

     The first rehearsal will be on            at            in

     Castleton Middle School Hall.

     Yours sincerely



     C Davies
     Producer

     Enc
```

ADVICE AND COMMENTS

As you can see this is a very straightforward task of putting information into the spaces provided. All the information is given in the question apart from the address of Miss Harvey. This can be taken from Task 3, as suggested.

The most difficult part of this task is to ensure that the information you insert is in alignment with the printed words of the line and that you set the work sensibly within the length of space allocated. Remember to leave at least one clear space after the last printed word before beginning your typing.

Do not forget that an envelope, addressed to Miss Harvey, is also required.

USEFUL FOLLOW-UP WORK

BUSINESS LETTERS   **TASK 1**

Type the following letter on A4 headed paper, taking a carbon copy.

Ref

Holden Products PLC
Crabtree Trading Estate
Colchester
Essex CO2 4PL

Dear Sirs

Order XL 5845

We hv to inform you that the goods ordered by us on 20 January have not yet arrived.
we ~~understand from~~ understood our recent
NP ~~in a recent⟋~~ telephone conversation that the parts were sent by
First-class post three days ago. [As you know, these parts are
stet needed to complete an order for a valued ~~customer~~ client + we really cannot wait any longer.

We suggest you despatch a replacement order by Data Post immediately since
L.C. Failure to receive the parts by the end of the week will seriously
⟋ damage ~~are good relations~~ the excellent business relationship we have built up over the past 5 years.

Yours ffy

John Bridgeman
Production Manager

You will recall a similar delay occured in completing our last order.

TASK 2

Type the following letter on headed paper. Take a carbon copy and address an envelope to Mr & Mrs Cartier.

Mr + Mrs H. Cartier
46 Melrose Gardens
Swindon SN9 4DT

Dear Mr + Mrs C,

We thank you for your letter of 26 May requesting details of our "Study" Holidays & hv pleasure in enclosing our current brochure. You wl notice th a wide variety of holidays are on offer, ~~which cover~~ ~~Covering~~ such interests + hobbies as photography, wildlife, ~~the~~ performing arts, architecture, history of art, walking, painting.

[stet] [list in alphabetical order]

Accommodation

Where available,
We use only 4-star hotels, + ensure all rooms hv private facilities. A single room supplement is charged in some cases.

Travel

This is by air from Gatwick Airport – economy class.

Courier Service

Each tour is accompanied by a courier who is also an "expert" in the subject to be studied however, visiting lecturers are engaged where necessary.

[O/wl]

(A — to be inserted here as sep para.)

(In the meantime)

We hope you wl. find a holiday to suit your interests + look forward to receiving your complete booking form. If we can be of any further assistance please do not hesitate to call.

[L.c.]

Yours sincerely
Premier Holidays Ltd

(A)
You will notice the nos. are restricted so that individual attention is given to each guest.

MEMORANDA **TASK 3**

Type a copy of the following, making all necessary corrections. Use the A5 memo form provided. Change times to 24 hour clock.

TO All Sales Reps   REF JR/yr *initials*

FROM Sales Director   DATE Today's

SALES MEETING

UC ' meeting of all sales (reps) *in full* will be held at (HO) on ~~Tuesday 14th March 1989~~ *in full Monday 5th March 1990*

UC commencing at 10 am. The meeting is expected to end by 4 pm. An agenda

will follow shortly.

,/ I those who travel a considerable distance//accommodation will be booked */overnight*

at the Crest Hotel, nearby. Please let me know/if you require ~~me to book a~~ *immed.* *such accom.*

~~room.~~

TASK 4

hrs/ To. Jon(h) Durdan
From Elain Walton

UC thanks for your recent memo regaurding the instalation of new
UC/N.P. machines in no 2workshop. I agree this will mean a certain
amount of disruption (&) suggest the work is carried out during
the weekend. *in full*

run on I know this will ma(e)n we shall have to pay a large amount of *hrs*
overtime to the enginears involved but feel this will be more *#*
cost affective than having production halted during the week.

,/ If you agree to my suggestion/please let me know which Dates *l.c*
would be most appropreate.

*Jenny: Could you retype this for me, please
I gave it to the new junior but
she didn't make a very good job
of it. Besides the corrections I've
noted, could you correct the spelling
errors I've underlined?*

Thanks
E W

TELEPHONE MESSAGES

TASK 5

a) Using a sheet of A5 paper, design a telephone message form, typing it with a carbon copy.

b) Remove from the typewriter and reinsert the CARBON COPY. Complete it with the following details:

Mrs Patton telephoned at 1430 today. She wished to speak to Mr Hall but he was out so you took the following message:

'I have found a suitable house and would like to move as soon as possible. Please let me know how you are proceeding with the legal work in respect of the sale of my present house.

I shall be at home tomorrow morning and would appreciate a telephone call.'

Mrs Patton's telephone number is 0942 652134

POSTCARDS

TASK 6

Type the following postcard. It is to be addressed (on the reverse side) to Greenlands Garden Centre, Bushy Road, Staines, Middx. TW18 4CH

HT White Ltd
209 Ferndale Street
WIGAN
Lancs.

Date as postmark

The garden ornaments as per your order No. 46935 will be despatched
                   Road Services
by British Rail on 26th November. Please advise us if they are not

received within two days of despatch.

COMPOSITION OF BUSINESS DOCUMENTS

BUSINESS AND PERSONAL LETTERS

IMPORTANT STEPS BEFORE TYPING

SUGGESTIONS FOR COMPOSING LETTERS

INTERNAL MEMORANDA

FORMAL INVITATIONS

ADVERTISEMENTS AND NOTICES

PRESS ADVERTISEMENTS

ANNOUNCEMENTS

GETTING STARTED

Skill in composing **business documents** is an important aspect of all examinations in typewriting and office communications, so you can almost certainly expect to be asked to compose a proportion of the correspondence in your coursework, and in the examination as well. This is the part of your course where you will be able to use your initiative and to demonstrate your ability beyond the basic copy-typing skill. You will still of course need to apply the *rules* you have learnt for displaying your document, but you will also have an opportunity to work things out for yourself, extracting information from several sources and communicating it in the form of letters, memos and so on.

The material for these documents would be given to you either:

a) as a **written instruction**, for example, in the form of a note outlining the reply to a letter

or

b) if you are taking an audio typewriting option, brief **spoken instructions** recorded on a tape.

Composing business documents, especially directly onto a typewriter, is not an easy task, and is one which requires as much practice as possible. However, when you do *not* have access to a typewriter, you could still work out *how* you would tackle this type of question. In this chapter we shall give you some advice on how to go about this.

ESSENTIAL PRINCIPLES

1 ▷ BUSINESS AND PERSONAL LETTERS

The type of letter you might be asked to write will probably fall into one of the following categories:

1 **Standard letters**, generally relating to the recruitment and selection of personnel, such as a letter inviting applicants to attend for an interview.

2 **Personal letters**, such as an application for a job in response to an advertisement.

3 **Covering letters**, for example, to a newspaper requesting the insertion of an advertisement or press release.

4 **Circular letters**. These could either be based on notes given in the question, or you could be asked to update a letter sent on a previous occasion.

5 **Letters of enquiry**. A letter such as this could arise in an assignment, when you might for example, be organising a social event, and have to write to caterers asking for a quotation. Alternatively, you might be given instructions to enquire about a specific item.

6 Letters either **requesting** a booking, say for hotel accommodation, or else **confirming** the reservation made.

7 **Replies to letters** - these are generally in response to a letter requesting information. The answer might be based upon notes given to you, or you might be expected to carry out some research, or you might need a combination of the two. You would probably be expected to refer to another task in the assignment, or to a separate document, for some of the information.

> 66 Identify the type of letter. This will help you to decide the tone to use 99

At the extended level you might expect to be asked to write:

8 **Letters of complaint**, or *reply to* a letter of complaint. You would probably be given notes on which to base your letter.

IMPORTANT STEPS BEFORE TYPING

Before you start typing your letter there are several important steps to take:

1 You should **read the instructions** very carefully - credit is given for following them, so it is well worth your while to spend a couple of minutes making sure you use the right size paper, produce the *correct number* of copies, and so on. You might find it useful to *highlight* or *underline* these points. If you are asked to refer to other documents you should then locate these and check their contents.

At the same time you should also establish the name and address of the person you are writing to, and equally important, check whether you will be signing the letter yourself, or have been asked to prepare the letter for someone else to sign.

> 66 Always read the instructions very carefully 99

2 You should then **decide** which of **the categories** 1 to 8 listed above the letter falls into:

   i) are you writing as a prospective customer, making a routine enquiry?

   ii) are you dealing with a complaint from a disgruntled customer? and so on.

This is important, as it will help you to **decide** on the 'tone' you should use.

3 Your next step is to jot down:

   i) a **check list** of the **basic items** you have to include in any business letter, making sure that they are in the correct order:

> 66 Some basic items to include in a business letter 99

- reference (if any)
- date
- name or title and address of addressee
- salutation (or opening)
- subject heading if appropriate
- complimentary close
- name and position of person who will be signing the letter

and, if these are relevant:

- 'Enc'
- 'Copies to'

ii) the **various points** you have been asked to make in the letter. This will help you to decide on a subject heading, and ensure that you do not forget any of the items.

You will probably gain a mark for each point you mention on your list, so you will find it well worthwhile to jot them all down.

4   You should now be ready to start typing your letter. Refer to your check list for the basic items, which you should key in as quickly and accurately as possible, to give yourself time for composing the letter itself. Try to get into the habit of working out each sentence and then typing it directly. Marks are given for style and use of English, so try to express yourself simply and in 'good' English. Avoid repeating the information given to you word for word.

SUGGESTIONS FOR COMPOSING LETTERS

> A good business letter should have an opening and a closing sentence

A good letter should start with a suitable **introduction**, referring to the main topic of the letter. If necessary the topic is developed in a further paragraph or paragraphs and should then end with an appropriate **closing sentence**. As the opening and closing sentences are fairly standard, it might help you to think of these beforehand. You will find some suggestions in Figure 6.1 to help you.

Some opening paragraphs

---

1   Letter of enquiry/request
    I am interested in your advertisement in . . .
    I should be grateful if you could send me . . .

2   Confirming arrangements
    Further to our telephone conversation (yesterday/this morning) I am writing to confirm . . .

3   Replying to a letter of enquiry
    Thank you for your letter of (date of letter) about/concerning (mention main subject of the letter)

4   Complaint
    My friends and I have just returned from a two week holiday in Spain on your Tour No IB 310, and we feel we must write and express our dissatisfaction.

5   Replying to a letter of complaint
    We were sorry to learn from our Branch Office that you were disappointed . . .
    We were very sorry to receive your letter of (date of letter) informing us that . . .

Some closing paragraphs

---

1   Letter of enquiry/request; also for a letter of complaint
    We look forward to receiving your reply/your comments/to hearing from you before the end of the week.

2   Confirming arrangements
    We look forward to meeting you next week

3   Replying to a letter of enquiry
    Please do not hesitate to contact me if you require any further information.

4   Complaint
    It would be helpful if we could meet to discuss this matter in more detail, and I would be grateful if you could suggest a date towards the end of the month, if this is convenient.

5   Replying to a letter of complaint
    In the meantime please accept our sincere apologies for the inconvenience we may have caused.
    We must apologise for any inconvenience this delay may cause you and hope that the arrangements we have made are satisfactory.

Fig. 6.1 Suggestions for composing letters

Figure 6.2 a) is an example of the type of task you might be asked to do in one of your coursework assignments. You are working as a Secretary/Receptionist in an hotel in Oxford. The Manager of the hotel, John Pickup, has asked you to answer the attached letter. From the notes given to you by Mr Pickup, type a reply to the letter for him to sign.

> **Remember to have an opening sentence, main paragraph and a closing sentence**

Before you start composing the letter, follow the procedures suggested earlier and then turn to Figure 6.2 b) to see how your checklist compares with the one in the figure. Figure 6.3 shows a worked example of the letter.

```
                                    5 Pelham Grove
                                       DALKEITH
                                      Midlothian
                                       EH22 6EL


          12 January 1989

          The Manager
          The Regent Hotel
          Oxford
          OX1 4SZ

          Dear Sir

          I am writing at the suggestion of some friends of ours, who
          stayed at your hotel last year and have thoroughly recommended
          it to us.

          My wife and I plan to spend a few days in Oxford and we would
          like to reserve a double room with bathroom en-suite from 28
          March to 4 April inclusive.  We would prefer to have a room
          with a balcony and if possible a view towards the river.

          I would be grateful if you could let me know whether you have
          a suitable room available, and what your rates would be for
          the above period.

          Yours faithfully

          M. Peters

          M. G. Peters
```

Please reply to mr Peters. Tell him we can let him have a double room with bathroom for period he wants but no balcony. The room is at the rear with good view of river and overlooking gardens. £40 per night for 2 (quote price for period, it includes VAT and breakfast.)

Fig. 6.2a) Letter and Notes

Fig 6.2 b) Checklist for reply to letter

Ref JP/NT
Date 19 January 1989
Addressee M Peters Esq
* and address*
Dear Mr Peters
Yours sincerely

Points to make:
✱ Double room w bathroom nights of 28 March to 4 April inclusive
✱ regret no balcony but at rear of hotel, overlooking gardens, river view
✱ Cost for 7 nights £280 inclusive of VAT and continental breakfast

Fig 6.3 Display of reply to Mr Peter's letter

The Regent Hotel
Oxford
OX1 4SX

Reference (John Pickup's initials/the secretary's)
Ref JP/NT

Today's date
16 January 1989

Name of Addressee
M G Peters, Esq
5 Pelhan Grove
DALKEITH

Address
Midlothian
EH22 6EL

Salutation
Dear Mr Peters

Opening sentence
Thank you for your letter of 12 January.

We shall be delighted to reserve a double room with bathroom en-suite for you and your wife for the nights of 28 March to 4 April inclusive. We regret the room does not have a balcony, but it is situated at the rear of the hotel, overlooking the gardens, with a fine view of the river. The cost for this suite for two persons for seven nights is £280 inclusive of VAT. This price includes a continental breakfast.

Closing sentence
We look forward to welcoming you to our hotel.

Complimentary close
Yours sincerely

Name and position of writer
John Pickup
Manager

2 ▶ INTERNAL MEMORANDA

Broadly there are two types of task involving the composition of a memo:

- those where you are asked to **look up information** and to pass it on in the form of a memo.
- those where you are instructed to **reply to a memo.** Your reply might be based upon notes given to you, or you might have to refer to other sources, such as a telephone message or letter.

The procedures for **composing a memo** are similar to those for a letter. As memos are used for communicating information to members within an organisation, they are *less formal* than a business letter. They should be *concise* and there is no need for the salutation and complimentary close; however, the tone you use should still always be *polite* and considerate.

You will probably be given a **memo form**. Make sure you use it – a mark may be lost for not doing so and it will also help to remind you to include the basic details:

'TO' and 'FROM' 'DATE' and 'REF'

each of which should gain you a mark if completed correctly.

Advice on composing a memo is on the same lines as for a letter:

> 5 points to remember when composing a memo

- read the instructions carefully
- jot down the points you will have to make
- complete the memo form, keying in the appropriate details
- type a subject heading (if appropriate)
- refer to your notes and type the main body of the memo.

Most candidates find the opening sentence the most difficult part of a memo to compose. Here again you might find it helpful to build up a collection of suitable openings.

3 FORMAL INVITATIONS

COMPOSING INVITATIONS

If you are asked to compose an invitation, this could either be in the form of:

a) a **circular letter**, containing details of the event, with a tear-off slip at the bottom of the letter. The invitation can be accepted or refused by completing the slip and returning it to the sender.

or

b) a **notice for display** announcing an event. These are considered in the section dealing with advertisements and notices.

Whatever the type of invitation, you will need to include the essential details:

- *Name* of the hosts or organisers
- *Purpose* or nature of the function
- *Date*, time and place.

REPLYING TO FORMAL INVITATIONS

> A good revision tip – make sure you know the formula for replying to invitations

Although you might be required to compose a formal invitation, you are most likely to be asked to reply formally to an invitation on behalf of your employer. Formal acceptances – and refusals – follow a set pattern. If you follow it, you will probably gain full marks, so it is well worth your while to have this formula at your fingertips.

The points to bear in mind are:

a) use the *third person*: 'Miss Smith' rather than 'I'
b) *thank* the sender
c) *repeat the details* given in the invitation
d) *accept* or *refuse* (giving a reason, if possible)
e) if included, the *date and address* of sender (it is optional) should go at the bottom of the reply.

Mr and Mrs Becket

JONATHAN BISHOP

requests the pleasure of your company
to a Buffet Lunch and Private Viewing
on Wednesday 24 May 1989
11.30 am to 3.30 pm
at The Roland Galleries
24 West Row
LONDON W1A 2CD

RSVP

Fig 6.4 Formal Invitation

Figure 6.4 is an example of a formal invitation which you might expect to answer. Compose the following:

i) an *acceptance*

ii) a *refusal* because Mr and Mrs Becket will be on holiday.

Then turn to Figures 6.5 a) and 6.5 b) to check your replies.

Mr and Mrs Becket thank Mr Jonathan Bishop for his kind

invitation to a Buffet Lunch and Private Viewing on

Wednesday 24 May 1989

at The Roland Galleries, 24 West Row, LONDON W1A 2CD

and have great pleasure in accepting

12 Pipers Lane

Bristol

BS17 30P

16 April 1989

Fig 6.5 a) Formal acceptance of an invitation

For the refusal, the first three points a) to c) would apply, so the wording would be the same as an acceptance, although there is no need to include the address of where the event will take place. The wording then would be:

. . . but regret that they are unable to attend as they will be away on holiday.

Mr and Mrs Becket thank Mr Jonathan Bishop for his kind

invitation to a Buffet Lunch and Private Viewing on

Wednesday 24 May 1989

at The Roland Galleries, 24 West Row, LONDON W1A 2CD

but regret that they are unable to attend as they will

be away on holiday

12 Pipers Lane

Bristol

BS17 30P

16 April 1989

Fig 6.5 b) Formal refusal of an invitation

There are two types of advertisements that you might be asked to prepare.

PRESS ADVERTISEMENTS

The most likely type would be an advertisement for a job vacancy to be placed in the classified section of a newspaper. You will probably be supplied with a description of the job and details of the type of person being sought, so the skill lies in presenting the essential details as briefly as possible in a logical order.

Here is a list of the *main items* which should be included in a **job advertisement**:

> 8 important items to include in a job advertisement

- job title
- location and type of work of company
- essential qualifications/qualities
- desirable qualifications/qualities
- age group
- salary and working conditions
- training offered (if relevant)
- how to apply.

One way of preparing for this type of task, is to:

a) collect three or four advertisements for a similar type of job
b) look critically at each advert, noting down the details, in the order in which they are given, on the lines shown in an advertisement in Figure 6.6
c) then – without looking at the original adverts, compose one of your own.

	JUNIOR SECRETARY
location and type of work of company	Would you like to work in a small but busy PR dept. in the West End of London?
Age group	We are looking for a bright college leaver, who would be willing to turn a hand to anything.
essential qualifications *desirable qualifications* *salary and working conditions*	Typing 40 wpm essential; knowledge of word processing useful. Friendly working atmosphere. Salary negotiable.
how to apply	Please telephone for further details or send your cv to: Brotherton & Co 112 Hyde Park Lane, London W1 Tel 251 9641.

Fig 6.6 A job advertisement

ANNOUNCEMENTS

These could involve, for example, the announcement of a forthcoming event, or a notice providing instructions on safety procedures. As with a classified advertisement, the details will most likely be given to you when you are set the task, although you might be asked to look up some of the data or to make a calculation.

To *prepare* an effective **announcement** you should:

- include all the information given to you
- choose the wording carefully, so that it is brief but can still be clearly understood
- display the announcement effectively.

This type of task gives scope for artistic skills, bearing in mind that it is a test of your typewriting as well.

EXAMINATION QUESTIONS

Here is a selection of questions taken from examinations set at the end of the course.

Question 1

Using the form provided, compose and type a memorandum from the General Sales Manager to the Regional Sales Manager (N. W. Region) informing him of the percentage increase and new salary rates for associates in that region.

The necessary information can be extracted from the schedule below. Information should be set out in tabular form with surnames in alphabetical order. Remind him that the new rates take effect from 31st July 1988.   (LEAG; 1988)

SALARY REVIEW

Salary Increases and new Scales for Associates

Effective from 31st July 1988

Name	Region	% Increase	New Salary £
Mr. R. Sondhi	S.W.	2	22,000
Mrs. L.Greenfield	N.W.	2	20,000
Ms. T. Waterman	N.W.	3	18,000
Mr. W. Symes	S.W.	4	12,500
Mrs. G. Fielding	N.E	1	24,000
Mr. A. Mohamed	S.E.	1	18,000
Miss Z. Barre	N.W.	3	14,500
Mrs. M. Gleen	S.E.	2	24,000
Mr. D. Thompson	N.W.	3	16,000
Mrs. I Francome	N.E.	4	10,000
Ms J. Butterfield	S.E.	4	14,000
Mr. A. Sonzogni	S.W.	3	10,500
Mr. L. Baroni	S.E.	3	11,500
Mr. R. Chudley	S.W.	1	13,000
Ms. N. Takaar	N.W.	1	12,500
Mr. F. Cartier	S.W.	2	21,000
Ms. B. Smallworthy	N.E.	4	21,500
Mr. T. Musto	London	1	19,000
Mr. S. Mistry	S.E.	3	18,000
Mr. F. Ferdinand	N.E.	3	17,000
Mr. I. Archibald	London	3	16,000
Mr. K. Nutwell	London	3	20,000
Mr. B. Jordan	London	4	18,000
Mr. A. Shori	N.E.	4	13,500
Mr. R. Bansal	N.W.	3	17,000

BUSINESS AND PERSONAL LETTERS

Question 2

In this question, candidates were asked to compose a letter based on material obtained from two other sources in the examination paper – the Background Information given at the beginning of the paper and a memo from the Secretary to the Producer, which they were required to type in an earlier task. For reasons of space we give only the relevant extracts from the Background Information and the memo.

Background Information
You have offered to help John Clark the secretary of your local amateur dramatic society, the Northchester Players, with some of the typing in preparation for the next production. You will need the following address: Northern Theatre, Park Road, Northchester, Lancashire, T66 7AB.

Extract from Memo

The auditions for parts for our autumn production of Bernard Shaw's 'Candida' have been arranged . . .

. . . The play will be performed for 6 evenings from Monday 7 November to Saturday 12 November commencing at 7.30 pm at the Northern Theatre, Northchester.

Task
Compose and type a letter to the Manager of the Northern Theatre confirming the booking of the theatre giving the dates and times of our performances. Let him know which play we are doing, that there are three Acts and that refreshments will be required during the Intervals. Use the A5 letterhead provided. You will need to refer to the memo in an earlier task for some of the information. (NEA; 1988)

Question 3

This question was set in the SEG Extended Option Paper. At this extended level, you will be expected to refer to other documents in the question paper when replying to a letter.

Task
Using the letter and the information below, compose and type a letter of reply to Mr Burnett. Use the fully blocked style.

Thank Mr Burnett for his booking and ask him to sign and return the Reservation booking form which you are enclosing. Ask him to forward a cheque for £50 as deposit.

Let him know that as soon as the form and deposit are returned you will send him confirmation of the booking, details of insurance and a note of the final amount payable for the holiday.

Include a paragraph in your letter to Mr Burnett giving brief details of the Deluxe Suite and the Outside Twin Cabins (see the extract from the Elite Group Holiday Cruises brochure) which are available on all ships.

The letter will be signed by Bridgette Curragh, Travel Consultant. Take a carbon copy of the letter.

Extract from the Elite Group Holiday Cruises brochure.

DELUXE SUITE – This is the most luxurious of our Staterooms and has the advantage of separate lounge and bedroom. The lounge has a veranda on the seaboard side. In a Deluxe Suite we ensure you receive the millionaire treatment!

OUTSIDE TWIN CABIN – Situated on either the Observation Deck or the Sun Deck, these cabins are luxuriously appointed and provide first-class accommodation. Each has its own special feature – your personal steward whom you will find to be a willing helper and a mine of useful information. (SEG; 1988)

Elite Group Holiday Cruises have received the following letter from Mr James Burnett.

46 Edward Road
Guildford
Surrey
GU6 5TX

10th May 1988

Dear Sir,

Cruise Holiday No. KHC/463 - 13 nights

Thank you for the information you sent recently on cruise holidays. I would like to confirm a booking for myself, wife Christine and my two daughters, Kate and Lucy, aged 12 and 8 respectively, on the above holiday. Could you please let me have further details of the types of accommodation available on board the ship.

We hope to join the ship at Southampton and would be grateful if you could arrange for the necessary car parking.

I would also be grateful for further details of the insurance cover offered by your company.

Yours faithfully

James Burnett.

(JAMES BURNETT)

Complete the Holiday reservation form

ADVICE AND COMMENTS: INTERNAL MEMORANDA

Question 1: Composing a memorandum

Make a note of the *instructions:*

■ use memo form provided
■ set out in a table with surnames in alphabetical order.

Your *checklist* should include:

- Who to?   Regional Sales Manager
                  (N. W. Region)
- Who from?   General Sales Manager
- Subject   Salary Review

Content

Since most of the content will consist of the table, your introductory paragraph will be important. Mention when the new rates take effect.

This question came at the end of the examination paper when candidates were probably running out of time – you should really allow yourself 25 minutes to do this task. Don't fall into the trap and lose even more time, by attempting to list all the names in the schedule – you are asked for those in the *N W Region only*: 6 out of the 25 listed! Remember to present them in alphabetical order.

ADVICE AND COMMENTS: BUSINESS AND PERSONAL LETTERS

Question 2: Composing a letter

Note the instructions:

- use A5 letterhead provided

Checklist

- reference   Ref: JC/(your initials)
- date   (Today's date)
- name and address   The Manager
  of addressee   Northern Theatre
                               Park Road
                               Northchester
                               Lancashire
                               T66 7AB
- Salutation   Dear Sirs
- Complimentary close   Yours faithfully
- Name and position of   John Clark
  author   Secretary of the
                               Northchester Players

Content

Confirm booking of theatre for 6 evenings from Monday 7 November to Saturday 12 November commencing at 7.30 pm for performance of George Bernard Shaw's 'Candida'. Three acts, refreshments required during the intervals.

Question 3: Composing a reply to a letter

Note the instructions:

- reply Mr James Burnett's letter
- use fully blocked style
- take a carbon copy
- enclose the Reservation booking form
- letter to be signed by Bridgette Curragh, Travel Consultant.

Draw up a *checklist* on the same lines as for the previous questions.

In addition to the information given to you in the question, you will need to refer to two other documents:

- the letter from Mr James Burnett
- the document about the Holiday Cruises.

A TUTOR'S ANSWER TO QUESTION 3

BUSINESS LETTERS

A reply to Mr James Burnett's letter.

```
Ref BC/nt

18 May 1988

J. Burnett Esq
46 Edward Road
GUILDFORD
Surrey
GU6 5TX

Dear Mr Burnett

Cruise Holiday No KHC/463 - 13 nights

Thank you for your letter of 10 May confirming your booking for
the above holiday for yourself, your wife and two daughters.  I
enclose a completed reservation form and would be grateful if
you could sign and return this to me, together with a cheque
for £50 as a deposit.

On receipt of your deposit and the reservation form duly
signed, I will send you confirmation of the booking, details of
insurance and a note of the final amount payable for your
holiday.

In reply to your query concerning accommodation, there are two
types available on board the ship:

DELUXE SUITE - This is the most luxurious of our Staterooms.
There is a separate lounge, with its own veranda on the
seaboard side, and bedroom.

OUTSIDE TWIN CABIN - Situated on either the Observation Deck or
the Sun Deck, these cabins are luxuriously appointed and
provide first-class accommodation.  Each deck has a steward who
will give personal service and attention.

I look forward to hearing from you in due course.

Yours sincerely



Bridgette Curragh
Travel Consultant

Encs
```

COURSEWORK ASSIGNMENTS

The first assignment contains tasks taken from Assignment B Secretarial tasks which were set in 1988 in the LEAG Coursework paper. These have to be completed towards the end of the two-year course in the fifth term, and you would be expected to take 15 to 20 minutes on each.

LEAG ASSIGNMENT B: SECRETARIAL TASKS

You work as Secretary to Mr B Copley of J Copley and Co., 325 Noble Street, London W4 3EC.

TASK 1 a)

Your firm wishes to replace two office staff who have left. From the following information produce a typed draft on an advertisement in blocked style.

We need a good junior copy typist who can preferably handle the switch board. I would prefer someone experienced rather than a school leaver, and I need proof of typing ability. We also need a junior to train as a receptionist; a school leaver who could type and do simple book-keeping would be ideal. Mention that we offer 4 weeks' annual holiday and supply luncheon vouchers. Salary is negotiable.   *(22 marks)*

TASK 1 b)

Type a letter to the London Evening Gazette, 249 Charlton Road, London, NW3 4LP, enclosing the advertisement. One insertion is required in the next issue of the paper.

(18 marks)

TASK 2

Refer to the Telephone Message Form. Type a memo to Mr L Dawson from Mr Copley, giving him the information about the word processor. Type another memo to Mrs G Corden telling her that the electronic typewriter will not be serviced as arranged. Two carbon copies of each memo are required, one copy marked for the file and one copy marked for Central Services.   *(22 marks)*

TELEPHONE MESSAGE

FOR Mr B Copley   TAKEN BY T E W

TIME 9.30 am   DATE 12-2-88

CALLER'S NAME Mr D Edwards

FIRM Coburn Equipment Ltd

ADDRESS 219 Barrington Avenue
        Nottingham   TELEPHONE NO 4358

Mr Edwards says he is unable to service the electronic typewriter today as promised, because the part required has not yet arrived. He will be coming next Monday at 2pm and he apologises for the inconvenience. He has obtained details of the word processor you enquired about and details are as follows:-

   MITSUNG PCP206 with printer and double disc drive -£860; can also get this with single disc drive for £730.

   He needs confirmation in writing if you want to order.

SEG COURSEWORK ASSIGNMENT

The next two tasks have been taken from one of the specimen assignments issued by the Southern Examining Group.

In Task 3 you are asked to type a covering letter for a press release, which is to be sent to the local newspaper as part of the publicity campaign for the play. When drafting the ticket in Task 4, you will need to refer to the press release for some of the details. You will find the full document in Chapter 4, page 41, of which the relevant details are:

'The performance is to be held in the Main School Hall beginning at 7.30 pm. and admission is by ticket which costs £1.50, available from the school office'.

You are the school secretary and work in the office of your local school. Students and staff are putting on a performance of the musical 'Oliver' on Saturday, 28 February 1989. The Head of Drama has asked you to carry out several tasks.

TASK 3

Prepare a covering letter, with a carbon copy, to go to the Editor of your local paper, enclosing the press release and asking him if he would publish it in the next edition of the paper. *(16 marks)*

Type an envelope for the letter. *(3 marks)*

TASK 4

Using the relevant information given in the press release, on suitable size paper, prepare a draft of a ticket to be used for the performance. Include on the ticket the information that refreshments will be available during the interval of the play. *(12 marks)*

OUTLINE ANSWERS

COURSEWORK ASSIGNMENTS

❝ Note the instructions, then draw up your checklist of key points ❞

ADVICE AND COMMENTS

Task 1a) Advertisement for 2 copy typists

Note the *instructions* first. These are:

- Draft advertisement
- Blocked style

Then draw up your *checklist* of key points.

The question will prompt you for most of the key points, but you will need to make it clear that you are advertising two separate posts with different requirements. Remember to include the method of applying as this is not mentioned in the question:

■ Name/Type or organisation	J Copley & Co
■ Name of job 1	Junior Copy Typist
■ Essential qualifications	GCSE Typing or equivalent knowledge of switchboard. Preferably experienced.
■ Name of job 2	Junior Receptionist
■ Essential qualifications	Ideally school leaver with ability to type and do simple book-keeping. Willingness to train as receptionist.
■ Salary/working conditions	Salary negotiable. 4 weeks' annual holiday; luncheon vouchers.
■ Method of application	Apply in writing to; Mr B Copley, 325 Noble St, London, W4 3EC

Task 1 b) Covering letter to the London Evening Gazette

You are not given any specific instructions, so you would have to decide the size of paper – A5 would be ideal. Use the headed notepaper provided.

Your checklist should be on these lines:

■ reference	Ref JB/(your initials)
■ date	(Today's date)
■ name and address of addressee	London Evening Gazette 249 Charlton Road LONDON NW3 4LP
■ Salutation	Dear Sirs
■ Complimentary close	Yours faithfully
■ Advertisement enclosed	Enc

Task 2 Composition of two memos

Take care when you have to prepare memos which have to be sent to different people, that you give the details to the correct person!

Start off by identifying from the instructions:

- who each memo is *from*
- who each memo is *going to*
- the main *content* of each memo
- the instructions regarding *copies*

Then refer to the telephone message for the details to be passed on. Your *checklist* should be on these lines:

1st Memo

■ Who to?	Mr Dawson
■ Who from?	Mr Copley
■ Number of copies?	2 copies cc to Central Services cc to file (Remember to type this information on the top copy!)
■ Subject	Mitsung PCP206

Main points: List the prices of the above.
Details from Mr Edwards of Coburn Equipment Ltd.
Confirmation of order in writing.

2nd Memo

■ Who to?	Mrs Corden
■ Who from?	Mr Copley's secretary (yourself)
■ Number of copies?	(as for Memo 1)
■ Subject	Servicing of electronic typewriter

Main points: Coburn Equipment Ltd have postponed until next Monday (give date) at 2 pm, as the part ordered has not arrived.

Remember to initial the memo with *your* initials.

Task 3 Covering letter for press release

You will need to look up the name and address of your local paper first.

Then jot down your check list of *basic items* for a letter (turn back to page 73 for this). Don't forget:

- a carbon copy is required

- to include 'Enc' at the bottom of the letter

- to type an envelope addressed to the Editor

Task 4 Ticket for 'Oliver'

Instructions

You are instructed to use 'suitable size paper'. If you can fit all the details onto a post card this would be a suitable size for a ticket.

Contents

Apart from the refreshments, you are not told what to include on the ticket, but as it is very similar to an invitation, check that you have the essential details for this (look back to page 41 if you can't remember what these are). In addition to these basic details, you should include the price of the ticket.

1 mark is awarded for each item you mention, so be sure to make all the points.

STUDENT ANSWERS WITH EXAMINER COMMENTS

TASK 3 COVERING LETTER FOR PRESS RELEASE

```
                   St George's County Upper School
                          Green Lane
                           OXFORD
Tel No Oxford 5242             OX1 6YT

20 January 1989

The Editor
Oxford & County Newspapers
Osney Mead
OXFORD
OX1 2BJ

Dear Sir

The pupils and staff of St George's County Upper School are
presenting the musical play 'Oliver' on Saturday
28th February 1989.

As in previous years, we would like to publicise the event
through your newspaper, and would appreciate it if you could
publish  the enclosed press release in the next edition of the
Oxford Times.

Yours sincerely




P White
Head of Drama


Enc
```

Be consistent over dates

The close should be 'Yours faithfully'

A good covering letter with only two errors

TASK 4 TICKET FOR 'OLIVER'

```
* * * * * * * * * * * * * * * * * * * * * * * *
*                                              *
*        ST GEORGE'S COUNTY SECONDARY SCHOOL   *
*                                              *
*                    presents                  *
*                                              *
*                  'O L I V E R'               *
*                                              *
*          Saturday 28 February 1989           *
*                                              *
*                   7.30 pm                    *
*                                              *
*              Main School Hall                *
*                                              *
*            Refreshments available            *
*              during the interval             *
*                                              *
* * * * * * * * * * * * * * * * * * * * * * * *
```

66 An attractive design, but the price of the ticket was omitted. The display is effective but time would have been better spent in checking that all the points have been included. 99

BUSINESS MEETING DOCUMENTS

NOTICE OF MEETINGS AND AGENDA

MINUTES

BUSINESS MEETING TERMS

GETTING STARTED

Besides knowing how to display the documents used at business meetings, you will also be expected, in all the examinations, to be able to compose a *notice* and *agenda* for a meeting. If you are taking the LEAG examination you will also be expected to know the more common terms used at meetings and to be able to summarise the proceedings. In any case it is helpful to be familiar with such terms and to develop your skills in summarising.

E S S E N T I A L   P R I N C I P L E S

1 ▷ NOTICE OF MEETINGS AND AGENDA

If you are asked to prepare a notice of a meeting and the agenda during your coursework, you may be given an example of the documents relating to a previous meeting and asked to update them. By the end of the course, you will be expected to know the standard contents and layout of these documents, so you might be given only the minimum of information. For example, you would probably be instructed to arrange a meeting and draw up an agenda 'using all the usual items'. In some questions you might be expected to refer to documents in other parts of the paper for one or more of the items.

You will find a list of the basic items which are usually found in a Notice and Agenda in Figure 7.1, but you may find it useful to draw up your own list and check with Figure 7.1 that you have these details at your fingertips.

Notice

Name of organisation (if any)
Title or type of meeting
Time, date and place of meeting
Date of issue
Name of person issuing the notice (usually the Secretary)

 A useful tip - always have a calendar in case you have to look up dates 🙶

Agenda

1   Apologies for absence
2   Minutes of previous meeting
3   Matters arising
4   Correspondence

5   (onwards)
    Numbered list of items for discussion (as agreed with the Chairman)
Last 2 items. Sometimes listed in the reverse order)

■ Any Other Business
■ Date of next meeting

Fig. 7.1   Basic items found in a typical Notice and Agenda

2 ▷ MINUTES

This topic is included in the syllabuses of the LEAG and MEG examinations and although, to date, tasks requiring the preparation of minutes have not often been set, this is a skill which could well be tested in the future.

The most likely way of doing this would be to present the candidate with an agenda used at a meeting, with notes jotted against the items which would have to be written up as minutes.

When writing formal minutes, there are several important points to bear in mind:

1   They should be **brief**, stating only the essential details.
2   They should be presented in the **order** in which the items on the agenda were dealt with and **numbered** accordingly.
3   They should be written in the **past tense** and in the **third person**. For example:

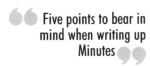 Five points to bear in mind when writing up Minutes 🙶

'Peter, I suggest that you go to the presentation on Monday and let us know how it went at our next meeting', could be written up as:

It was suggested that Peter Stewart should go to the presentation on the following Monday and report back to the Committee at the next meeting.
4   They should be **easy to understand**. One way of testing the clarity of the minutes is to check that they are clearly understood not only by the members who were present at the meeting, but also by those who did not attend it.
5   They should be absolutely **accurate**, particularly when recording a decision that has been reached.

3   BUSINESS MEETING TERMS

When you are writing up minutes, you would find it useful to know the more common business meeting terms. In their syllabus, LEAG lists 16 of these terms which candidates are expected to be able to use (see Fig. 7.2 a)).

a) ad hoc	i) point of order
b) AGM	j) proposer
c) amendment	k) proxy
d) ballot	l) quorum
e) casting vote	m) resolution
f) lie on the table	n) rider
g) minute book	o) seconder
h) nem con	p) sine die

Fig 7.2 a) 16 committee terms

You could check how well you know the terms by looking at the eight definitions in Figure 7.2 b) and then selecting from among the terms in Figure 7.2 a) the one which you think is being described. The first one has been done for you, and you will find the answers to the others at the end of the next section in Figure 7.2 c).

1   a second vote allowed to the chairman in the event of a deadlock – e)
2   for an indefinite period
3   a motion passed by a majority vote
4   an alteration to a motion
5   a motion presented to a meeting, but no action was taken on it
6   an addition to a resolution that had already been passed
7   a query raised by a member regarding the conduct of the meeting
8   no one opposed a motion, but everyone voted.

Fig 7.2 b) Eight definitions of business meeting terms

COURSEWORK ASSIGNMENTS

LEAG ASSIGNMENT A: LOCAL YOUTH CLUB

This task and the final one were set in the LEAG Coursework paper 2 (Assignment A) in 1989. The tasks in this assignment have to be completed in the fourth term of a two-year course.

TASK 1

You have had to give up the post of Secretary to the Club. The new person, who will take over from you, is unaware of some of the terms and procedures for meetings and has asked you to explain these to him.

Set out brief notes, which can be passed on to him, on the following points:

    i) the meanings of:
        ad hoc
        ex officio
        quorum
    ii) the items of information which should be included in a notice of meeting
    iii) the set items which would appear on a committee meeting agenda   *(20 marks)*

SEG COURSEWORK ASSIGNMENT

The next two tasks have been taken from a specimen coursework assignment issued by the Southern Examining Group.

You have taken over as temporary secretary to the Chairman of a firm of solicitors. One of your tasks is to deal with the paperwork and booking of meetings. Fortunately, his usual secretary keeps an efficient file of specimen layouts.

TASK 2

Using the specimen Notice of Meeting, prepare an up-to-date copy for today's date. The Development Sub-Committee Meeting will be in the usual place two weeks from today, starting at 10.30 am. *(13 marks)*

Specimen Notice of Meeting for use with Task 2

AYLESWOOD SOLICITORS
17 Old Lane
HULL
HU6 9TB

Chairman
J Ayleswood

Secretary:
P Ayleswood

9th December 1989«

A meeting of the Development Sub-Committee will be held in the Committee Room, Chamber of Commerce, on 19th December 1988 at 2 pm.

J Goodwin (Miss)
SECRETARY

TASK 3

Compile the Agenda for the above meeting using all the standard acceptable items, for example, Apologies for Absence. The one major item for discussion is:

Siting of the new hypermarket.

As it is anticipated that this item will take a long time to discuss, the meeting will need a mid-day break. *(24 marks)*

LEAG ASSIGNMENT A: AMATEUR DRAMATIC SOCIETY

This task was set in the LEAG Coursework paper 2 (Assignment A) in 1988. In this examination, candidates are expected to refer to a separate inset booklet, containing additional information.

TASK 4

You are undertaking secretarial work for an Amateur Dramatic Society.

You have received the enclosed memo from the Producer regarding preparations for the next meeting of The Villages ADS Committee. From the information it contains, prepare the Notice of Meeting and Agenda. Type 'New Members' before details of the next production. Include all the normal items of business, together with the items mentioned in the enclosed memo.

(The memo, with the list of members and synopsis of plays is printed as a separate inset booklet)

Information for Task 4

TO: Secretary   **REF:** CD

FROM: Producer   **DATE:** 14 November 1987

COMMITTEE MEETING

look up date → Just a reminder for you – meeting will be on first Monday in December in Castleton Middle School Hall. *7 30 pm*

Items raised at the last meeting will be discussed and the usual financial reports. Other items –

```
Next production - (a) Royal Hunt of the Sun
(b) King Lear (c) A Midsummer Night's Dream (d) The
Wind in the Willows

New members

Logo - 3 designs received from members

Publicity

Printing - tickets and programmes

I shall also make a report.

I attach a list of new members and a synopsis of each
play for reading.  If you type a copy of each and let
me have all the material as soon as possible - I'll
arrange to have it duplicated for distribution at the
meeting.
```

LEAG ASSIGNMENT 'A: LOCAL YOUTH CLUB

TASK 5

Here is the second task taken from the same paper as Task 1, where the student is the Secretary to the Local Youth Club.

Type up the Minutes of the recent committee meeting held on 16th November. Please take a carbon copy.

Minutes of Entertainments Committee Meeting held in the Church Hall at 7.30pm on 16th November 1988

Present: Mrs Jean Browne (in the chair)
? (your name) (Secretary)

Please list
these in
alphabetical
order
{ Satvir Patel
Rajesh Bansal
Maureen Kirkpatrick
Paul Strong

Apologies: An apology was received from Jean Graham

Minutes: The Minutes of the meeting held on 20th October were read, approved and signed by the Chairman.

Matters arising: There were no matters arising from these Minutes.

Christmas Disco: Satvir reported that the hall had been booked and confirmation received from High Life Disco. Maureen reported that she had recruited 4 volunteers to help provide and sell refreshments. It was decided to make a final effort to sell more tickets, particularly at the next club meeting.

Fund raising projects: It was decided to put up a list in the hall asking for suggestions. Further discussion was deferred until the next meeting.

Summer Camp: It was agreed that there was evidence of strong support for this from club members. After much discussion Paul and Maureen agreed to make enquiries about possible locations and approximate costs for a week's camp in July next. They agreed to report back to the next meeting.

A.O.B: ? (your name) indicated that she may have to relinquish her position as club secretary after Christmas as she is leaving the district.

Date of next meeting: This was fixed for ? (insert date – 3rd Wed. of Jan!).

Answers

Definition 1	matches e) 'casting vote'
Definition 2	matches p)
Definition 3	matches m)
Definition 4	matches c)
Definition 5	matches f)
Definition 6	matches n)
Definition 7	matches i)
Definition 8	matches h)

Fig 7.2 c) Answers to the definitions in Fig 7.2 b)

OUTLINE ANSWERS TO TASKS 1–5

COURSEWORK ASSIGNMENTS

ADVICE AND COMMENTS

Task 1: Notes on terms and procedures at meetings

i) When marking this type of question, the examiner will be looking for key words in your definition. These have been highlighted in the suggested answer:

ad hoc   a **committee** formed to deal with one **specific piece of work**. Once completed the committee is disbanded.

ex officio   a person who is **a member** of a committee by **virtue of his** or **her office**.

quorum   the **minimum number** of **members** of a committee who must be **present** for the meeting to take place. The quorum is specified in the rules of the constitution.

ii) Items to be included in a notice of meeting and

iii) Set items which would appear on an agenda

These are listed in Figure 7.1. Make sure you know them, as you will find it useful to be able to recall the list when tackling Tasks 3 and 4.

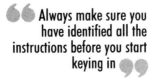 Always make sure you have identified all the instructions before you start keying in

Task 2: Notice of Meeting

Note the instructions first. These are:

■ Type a notice of a meeting of the Development Sub-Committee.

■ Refer to the example of a notice of a previous meeting and change the date of the meeting to two weeks from today and the time to 10.30 am.

■ Date the Notice with today's date.

Advice: Copy the specimen Notice exactly as you see it, but take care to alter both dates and the time - three items in all.

Task 3: Compiling an Agenda

Remember that an agenda consists of three main sections, so you could start of by jotting down the details you have been given under the different sections. Refer back to your answer to Task 1 ii) and iii) to check that you have remembered to include all the set items:

1   The date, time and place etc of the meeting. These details are in the Notice of the Meeting in Task 2.
2   The six standard items on an agenda. You are given the first - Apologies for Absence, so jot down the other three you would expect to be dealt with at the beginning of the meeting, and the final two.
3   The variable items. In this case there is just one. Remember to indicate the break for lunch.

You will find a student's answer to Tasks 2 and 3 on pages 97–8.

Task 4: Compiling a Notice of Meeting and Agenda

This task is more difficult than the previous ones, as you have to identify the various items mentioned in the memo, and then arrange them according to the instructions.

Advice: Make a note of the instructions. These are to prepare:

❝ Refer to a calendar when looking up the date ❞

1   The Notice of the next Meeting.
    This could be done fairly quickly. You will find the name of the Committee in the instructions, and the memo will tell you the place and time. The only thing you will have to look up is the first Monday in December for the date.
2   The Agenda.
    List the usual items first. Then go carefully through the memo from the Producer, underlining the various points which you are asked to list. You will find an example of how you could do this in Figure 7.3.
    When you come to list the items, refer back to the question, and check the instructions regarding the order in which these additional items should be listed.

TO: Secretary   REF: CD

FROM: Producer   DATE: 14 November 1987

COMMITTEE MEETING

Look up date — Just a reminder for you – meeting will be on first
Monday in December in Castleton Middle School Hall. — *7.30pm*

Items raised at the last meeting will be discussed
and the usual <u>financial reports</u>. Other items –
          5   *5. Treasurer's Report.*

8. <u>Next production</u> – (a) Royal Hunt of the Sun
   (b) King Lear (c) A Midsummer Night's Dream
   (d) The Wind in the Willows

7. <u>New members</u>

9. <u>Logo</u> – 3 designs received from members

❝ Make a note of the first 4 items and the last 2, and then underline the other topics which will be on the agenda ❞

10. <u>Publicity</u>

11. <u>Printing</u> – tickets and programmes

I shall also make a <u>report</u>.   *6 Producer's Report*

I attach a list of new members and a synopsis of each
play for reading. If you type a copy of each and let
me have all the material as soon as possible – I'll
arrange to have it duplicated for distribution at the
meeting.

Fig. 7.3 Identification of items for the agenda

Task 5: Typing up the Minutes of the committee meeting

Remember to read through the *whole* passage before attempting to commence typing. The handwriting is quite clear but there are several extra pieces of information to insert and the names have to be rearranged in alphabetical order.

Note that a carbon copy is required. This is rather a long passage and so you are advised to decide on the layout well in advance and to commence typing slowly so that you will not have to keep stopping to erase errors on the carbon copy.

Although there is no specific instruction to do so, you would be well advised to type A.O.B in full.

You are not told which method of layout to use. There are basically two methods:

a) The blocked style - which should incorporate open punctuation.
b) The standard style - which may have closed, or standard, punctuation.

A Tutor's answer for this task, in both styles, is included in the final section.

STUDENT ANSWER TO TASKS 2 AND 3 AND EXAMINER COMMENTS

TASK 2: NOTICE OF MEETING

AYLESWOOD SOLICITORS
17 Old Lane
HULL
HU6 9TB

Chairman: Secretary:
J Ayleswood   P Ayleswood **66 Align 99**

66 Development omitted. 99

                        20th March 1990 ⟶

A meeting of the ⌇Sub-Committee will be held in the Committee
Room, Chamber of Commerce, on 3rd April 1989 at 10.⟨00⟩ am. **66 Wrong time. 99**

                         J Goodwin (Miss)
                         SECRETARY

66 There are costly errors in this short task. Take great care, as you type, to include every word - it is impossible to insert a long word like 'Development' afterwards! **99**

TASK 3: COMPILING AN AGENDA

AYLESWOOD SOLICITORS

The Development Sub-Committee will be holding their meeting in the Committee Room, Chamber of Commerce, on 3rd April 1989 at 10.30 am.

A G E N D A

1   Apologies for absence

2.   Minutes of the previous meeting

3   Matters arising from the minutes   66 Initial caps 99

4   Correspondance   66 Spelling! 99

5   Siting of the new hypermarket

12.30   LUNCH

Siting of the new hypermarket
(discussion to be continued after lunch)

6.   Any other business

7   Date and time of the next meeting

66 Full marks for display and content - this candidate remembered to include the lunch break in the middle of the meeting too. 99

A TUTOR'S ANSWER TO TASKS 4 AND 5

TASK 4: COMPILING A NOTICE OF MEETING AND AGENDA

66 If you are given no specific instructions on layout, you can decide for yourself whether you want to use 'blocked' or 'standard' style. 99

The Villagers Amateur Dramatic Society

The next meeting of the Villagers Amateur Dramatic Society Committee will take place on Monday 6 December 1987 in Castleton Middle School Hall at 7.30 pm.

A G E N D A

1   Apologies for absence
2   Minutes of the previous meeting
3   Matters arising from the Minutes
4   Correspondence
5   Treasurer's report
6   Producer's report
7   New members. A list will be circulated at the meeting

8   Next production. The following plays will be considered:
   a) Royal Hunt of the Sun
   b) King Lear
   c) A Midsummer Night's Dream
   d) The Wind in the Willow
   A synopsis of each play will be distributed at the meeting
9   The new logo. To consider 3 designs received from members
10 Publicity
11 To discuss the printing of programmes and tickets
12 Date and time of the next meeting
13 Any other business

Hon Secretary   16 November 1987

TASK 5: TYPING UP THE MINUTES OF A COMMITTEE MEETING

Minutes of Entertainments Committee Meeting held in
the Church Hall at 7.30 p.m. on 16th November 1988.

Present:

Mrs. Jean Browne (in the Chair)
Jenny White   (Secretary)
Rajesh Bansal
Maureen Kirkpatrick
Satvir Patel
Paul Strong

Apologies:	An apology was received from Jean Graham.
Minutes:	The Minutes of the meeting held on 20th October were read, approved and signed by the Chairman.
Matters arising:	There were no matters arising from these Minutes.
Christmas Disco:	Satvir reported that the hall had been booked and confirmation received from High Life Disco. Maureen reported that she had recruited four volunteers to help provide and sell refreshments. It was decided to make a final effort to sell more tickets, particularly at the next club meeting.
Fund raising projects:	It was decided to put up a list in the hall asking for suggestions. Further discussion was deferred until the next meeting.
Summer Camp:	It was agreed that there was evidence of strong support for this from club members. After much discussion Paul and Maureen agreed to make enquiries about possible locations and approximate costs for a week's camp in July next. They agreed to report back to the next meeting.
Any other business:	Jenny White indicated that she may have to relinquish her position as club secretary after Christmas as she is leaving the district.
Date of next meeting:	This was fixed for 18th January 1989.

a) Standard layout with closed punctuation

MINUTES of Entertainments Committee Meeting held in the Church Hall at 7.30 pm
on 16 November 1988.

PRESENT

Mrs Jean Browne (in the Chair)
Jenny White   (Secretary)
Rajesh Bansal
Maureen Kirkpatrick
Satvir Patel
Paul Strong

Apologies	An apology was received from Jean Graham.
Minutes	The Minutes of the meeting held on 20 October were read, approved and signed by the Chairman.
Matters arising	There were no matters arising from these Minutes.
Christmas Disco	Satvir reported that the hall had been booked and confirmation received from High Life Disco. Maureen reported that she had recruited four volunteers to help provide and sell refreshments. It was decided to make a final effort to sell more tickets, particularly at the next club meeting.
Fund raising projects	It was decided to put up a list in the hall asking for suggestions. Further discussion was deferred until the next meeting.
Summer Camp	It was agreed that there was evidence of strong support for this from club members. After much discussion Paul and Maureen agreed to make enquiries about possible locations and approximate costs for a week's camp in July next. They agreed to report back to the next meeting.
Any other business	Jenny White indicated that she may have to relinquish her position as club secretary after Christmas as she is leaving the district.
Date of next meeting	This was fixed for 18 January 1989.

b) Fully-blocked style with open
         punctuation

Comments on the layout of the Minutes
You will notice in the example of the fully-blocked style, that the dates have been
represented as 20 October and 18 January. With open punctuation it is common practice to
omit the 'th' in the date. However, it is unlikely that 20th and 18th would be penalized.
Notice in the Minute on the Christmas Disco that 'four' has been written as a word. The
figure '4' could have been used, as in the manuscript, but if in doubt, it is as well to
represent a number below 10, which is on its own in text, as a word rather than a figure.

There is no specific position for the word 'Present' in the Minutes. It would have been
just as acceptable to have placed it as a side heading as in the draft.

**If in doubt type
abbreviations in full, and a
single figure below the
number 10 as a word**

GETTING STARTED

In an office, the smooth flow of information is crucial to its successful operation. So the ability to extract, compile and interpret information and then to present it effectively, is a valuable skill, and one which is fundamental to the course.

Whenever you carry out a task, you will be getting some practice in interpreting instructions and, in most cases, practice in deciding how to present the information as effectively as possible.

In this chapter we shall look at the main **sources of information**, both traditional and computerized, that you might be expected to use when carrying out coursework assignments. We shall also consider the preparation of **itineraries**, as this is one of the key tasks involving research and compilation of information.

SOURCES OF INFORMATION

MAIN SOURCES

ITINERARIES

BASIC REFERENCE BOOKS

COMPANY RECORDS

COMPUTERIZED SOURCES OF INFORMATION

ITINERARIES

PLANNING A JOURNEY

COMMENTS ON THE RESEARCHING QUESTION

TYPING THE ITINERARY

ESSENTIAL PRINCIPLES

1 > MAIN SOURCES

The main sources of information that you should know how to use are:

BASIC REFERENCE BOOKS

These are still an important source of information in the office and you should have plenty of opportunity of using them throughout your course.

A good **dictionary** is essential, both in helping you to check spelling and to find out the meaning of words. You will also find a list of the more common abbreviations. As you are permitted to refer to a dictionary in an examination, try to get as much practice as you can in using one, so that you can locate words as quickly as possible when under pressure.

> **Get as much practice as you can in looking facts up speedily and accurately. In business, information that arrives too late is worthless information**

When composing correspondence, if you get stuck for the right word or wish to avoid repetition of the same word, try *Roget's Thesaurus* – if you haven't used a thesaurus before, you may need a little practice. A book on the use of English, such as *Fowler's Modern English Usage* will help you to express yourself correctly.

Black's Titles and *Forms of Address*, or a similar publication, gives advice on the correct way to address a correspondent with a title.

LEAG recommends several books, which include, in addition to those mentioned above, the *Post Office Guide,* the *Telecom Guide* and *Whitaker's Almanack.*

Several of the SEG coursework tasks require some research for local information from the *Yellow Pages* and *Thompson Guides.*

Reference books providing travel information are considered in the section on itineraries.

COMPANY RECORDS

Files containing records of a company's correspondence and communications, form the basis of any business information system, and it is important to gain practice in extracting relevant details from these records. As we see in Chapters 6 and 7, you will quite often need to refer to other documents when composing correspondence.

COMPUTERIZED SOURCES OF INFORMATION

This is information stored on a computer disk known as a **database**. Although you would not be expected to use computerized sources of information in the current typewriting examinations, you should be aware of the two main types:

a) the **private databases** which hold the records of a company
b) the information services available to the general public known under the general name of Videotex. The main ones which you should know about are:

> **Teletext:** The one-way TV information service provided by BBC (Ceefax) and ITV (Oracle)
> **Viewdata:** Information service such as Prestel linking TV or computers by telephone to a central database enabling two-way exchange of information.
> **Closed User Groups** which provide a private specialist information service between subscribers to the particular group.

2 > ITINERARIES

These are summaries of travel arrangements, hotel reservations and business meetings. You will almost certainly have an opportunity of preparing an itinerary in your coursework, and possibly in the examination as well.

You might be given most of the details and asked to refer to, say, an airline schedule, and to look up a suitable flight, or you might be instructed to make all the arrangements for a business trip. In either case you will, of course, be expected to present your itinerary in a manner that is clearly understood.

PLANNING A JOURNEY

You should be aware of the main sources of information when making travel arrangements.

The two main ones that you are advised to get practice in using are:

1   **AA or RAC Handbooks**. These supply not only a list of recommended hotels in every town in the UK, but also detailed information about road travel – distances, maps and motorways – to help with route planning both in the UK and overseas.

2   **Rail** Timetables, **Airline** Schedules and **Car Ferry** Timetables. In a timed examination you may be given an extract from the appropriate timetable and asked to look up a suitable flight or arrange a train journey. There is so much information packed into these timetables, that you will need practice in using them; in the examination itself, allow yourself sufficient time to check the notes and the meaning of the light and heavy print.

You will find some guidelines in Figure 8.1 on arranging a rail journey to a meeting. They could apply equally well to the arrangements for a flight.

Note: Although morning and afternoon times are still referred to as 'am' and 'pm' especially when people are speaking, all timetables use the 24-hour system, and as the timings of an itinerary should also be presented in this manner, it is essential that you practise converting the times to the continental system. Just add 12 to the pm time. For example:

3 pm is 3 + 12 = 1500 hours
9 pm is 9 + 12 = 2100 hours

---

1   Work out your timings backwards from the time when the meeting starts.

2   Find out how long it will take to get from the station to the place where the meeting is being held.

3   Use a ruler when looking up the train times, and remember to check the *Notes* to find out the meanings of symbols.

> Allow some extra time in case of delays on the rail – nobody likes to rush into a meeting unprepared!

4   Select a train which arrives at the destination in good time.

5   Bear in mind any specific instructions and constraints, such as:

■ the earliest time the traveller can leave for the meeting

■ requirements with regard to restaurant or buffet facilities

■ wishes concerning 1st class travel – not all trains offer this.

6   When you have found the time of a train which appears to be suitable, check from the small print that it is running on that day – there are exceptions on weekdays, and these are not only on Saturdays.

7   If you have a choice of trains which satisfy the above criteria, select the one

■ that does not involve a change

■ which will take the least amount of time to cover the distance. Sometimes a train which leaves slightly later, will arrive before an earlier one.

Fig. 8.1 Some guidelines on arranging a rail journey to a meeting

Below is a typical question where you are asked to refer to an extract from a railway timetable and look up a suitable train. At first sight there appears to be more than one option, but if you follow the guidelines, you will find that the choice is rather more limited. When you have done this check your answer with the comments which follow.

Question:

You work at the London Head office of a firm of accountants. One of the partners, Owen Morris, has to attend a meeting at one of the branch offices in Cardiff next Monday 22 May. The meeting is due to start at 12.00 noon and carry on over lunch. It is anticipated that the business will be completed by mid-afternoon, at about 3.30 pm. The branch office is 10 minutes by taxi from Cardiff Central Station. Mr Morris must be back in London (Paddington) that evening, at the very latest by 7.00 pm, preferably earlier.

London—Bath—Bristol—Cardiff—Swansea

MONDAYS TO FRIDAYS

		†	IC⊘	IC⊘	IC✕	IC✕	IC⊘	IC⊘
London Paddington	d	—	—	0700	0720	0800	0810	0830	0840
Slough	d	—	—	0714	0734	0748	—	—	0854
Gatwick Airport	d	—	—	—	—	0637	—	—	0717
Heathrow Airport	d	—	—	—	—	0655	—	0725	—
Reading	d	—	—	0728	0748	0825	0834	0854	0908
Didcot Parkway	d	—	—	0739	0759	—	—	—	0919
Swindon	a	0645	0733	0759	0819	—	0901	0921	0939
Chippenham	a	0701	0749	—	0832	—	—	0934	—
Bath Spa	a	0715	0804	—	0843	—	0921	0945	—
Bristol Parkway	a	—	—	0823	—	0910	—	—	1003
Bristol Temple Meads	a	0733	0823	—	0858	—	0936	1000	—
Weston-super-Mare	a	0754	0853	—	0947	—	—	1028	—
Newport	a	—	—	0845	—	0933	—	—	1025
Hereford	a	—	—	0957	—	1107	—	—	—
Cardiff Central	a	—	—	0902	—	0950	—	—	1042
Bridgend	a	—	—	—	—	1010	—	—	—
Port Talbot Parkway	a	—	—	—	—	1022	—	—	—
Neath	a	—	—	—	—	1030	—	—	—
Swansea	a	—	—	—	—	1043	—	—	—

		IC✕	IC✕	G IC⊘	IC⊘	IC⊘	IC⊘	IC✕	IC⊘
London Paddington	d	0900	0905	0930	0950	1000	1010	1030	1043
Slough	d	0900	—	—	0943	—	—	—	1044
Gatwick Airport	d	—	—	—	0822	—	—	0922	—
Heathrow Airport	d	0755	—	0825	—	0855	—	0925	—
Reading	d	0925	0931	0954	—	1024	1035	1058	1107
Didcot Parkway	d	—	—	—	—	—	—	1109	—
Swindon	a	—	0958	—	—	1051	—	1129	1136
Chippenham	a	—	1011	—	—	—	—	1142	—
Bath Spa	a	—	1022	—	1052	—	—	1153	—
Bristol Parkway	a	1009	—	—	—	1117	1123	—	—
Bristol Temple Meads	a	—	1037	—	1107	—	1133	1208	—
Weston-super-Mare	a	—	1059	—	1151	—	—	1234	—
Newport	a	1031	—	—	—	1137	—	—	—
Hereford	a	1212	—	—	—	1305	—	—	—
Cardiff Central	a	1047	—	—	1110	1153	—	—	—
Bridgend	a	1107	—	—	—	1213	—	—	—
Port Talbot Parkway	a	1119	—	—	—	1225	—	—	—
Neath	a	1126	—	—	—	1232	—	—	—
Swansea	a	1139	—	—	—	1245	—	—	—

		IC✕	IC⊘	IC⊘	IC⊘	IC✕	IC⊘	IC⊘	IC✕
London Paddington	d	1100	1130	1200	1230	1300	1330	1400	1430
Slough	d	—	1144	—	1244	—	1323	1336	1444
Gatwick Airport	d	—	1026	—	1126	—	1226	1326	—
Heathrow Airport	d	0955	1025	1055	1125	1155	1225	1255	1325
Reading	d	1125	1158	1224	1258	1324	1354	1424	1458
Didcot Parkway	d	—	1209	—	1309	—	—	1405	1509
Swindon	a	1152	1229	1251	1329	1351	1425	1451	1529
Chippenham	a	—	1242	—	—	1342	—	—	1542
Bath Spa	a	—	1254	—	—	1353	—	1445	1553
Bristol Parkway	a	1216	—	1315	—	1415	—	1515	—
Bristol Temple Meads	a	—	1308	—	1408	—	1500	—	1608
Weston-super-Mare	a	—	1344	—	1451	—	1522	1630g	1651
Newport	a	1238	—	1337	—	1437	—	1537	—
Hereford	a	1351	—	1505	—	1605	—	1703	—
Cardiff Central	a	1254	—	1353	—	1453	—	1553	—
Bridgend	a	1314	—	1414	—	1514	—	1614	—
Port Talbot Parkway	a	1326	—	1426	—	1526	—	1626	—
Neath	a	1333	—	1433	—	1533	—	1633	—
Swansea	a	1346	—	1446	—	1546	—	1646	—

Fig. 8.2 a) InterCity London–South Wales; Guide to Services

London—Bath—Bristol—Cardiff—Swansea

MONDAYS TO FRIDAYS—continued

		FO IC⊘	IC⊘	IC⊘	IC⊘	IC✕	IC⊘	IC⊘	IC⊘
London Paddington	d	1455	1500	1530	1600	1605	1635	1645	1700
Slough	d	—	—	1544	—	—	1625	—	1636
Gatwick Airport	d	—	—	—	—	1426	—	1526	—
Heathrow Airport	d	—	1355	1425	—	1455	1525	—	1555
Reading	d	—	1524	1558	—	1629u	1659u	1709u	1724u
Didcot Parkway	d	—	—	1609	—	—	—	1721	—
Swindon	a	1543	1551	1629	1647	1656	1728	1741	1751
Chippenham	a	—	—	1642	—	1709	1752	—	1804
Bath Spa	a	—	—	1653	—	1720	—	—	1815
Bristol Parkway	a	1610s	1615	—	1711	—	1750	—	—
Bristol Temple Meads	a	1625	—	1708	—	1735	—	—	1830
Weston-super-Mare	a	1713	—	1745	—	1818	—	—	1900
Newport	a	—	1638	—	1733	—	1812	—	—
Hereford	a	—	1757	—	1846	—	1910	—	—
Cardiff Central	a	—	1653	—	1749	—	1828	—	—
Bridgend	a	—	1714	—	1810	—	1849	—	—
Port Talbot Parkway	a	—	1726	—	1822	—	1901	—	—
Neath	a	—	1733	—	1829	—	1908	—	—
Swansea	a	—	1746	—	1844	—	1921	—	—

		A IC⊘	IC⊘	IC⊘	IC⊘P	FX IC	FO IC	FO IC	IC⊘
London Paddington	d	1720	1730	1740	1759	1805	1807	1807	1823
Slough	d	1705	—	—	—	1750	—	—	—
Gatwick Airport	d	—	—	—	—	1622	—	—	—
Heathrow Airport	d	1625	—	—	—	1655	—	—	—
Reading	d	1745u	—	—	1811	1829u	—	1837u	—
Didcot Parkway	d	—	—	1811	—	—	1847	1852	—
Swindon	a	1812	1817	1832	—	1856	1911	1916	1921
Chippenham	a	—	1830	—	—	1909	—	—	1934
Bath Spa	a	—	1841	—	—	1921	—	—	1945
Bristol Parkway	a	1838	—	—	1909	—	1950m	1950	—
Bristol Temple Meads	a	—	1856	—	—	1936	—	—	2000
Weston-super-Mare	a	—	1938	—	—	2005	—	—	—
Newport	a	1900	—	—	1931	—	2018m	2018	—
Hereford	a	2005	—	—	2118	—	—	—	—
Cardiff Central	a	1917	—	—	1947	—	2034m	2034	—
Bridgend	a	1938	—	—	2007	—	2057m	2057	—
Port Talbot Parkway	a	1950	—	—	2019	—	2113m	2113	—
Neath	a	1958	—	—	2026	—	2121m	2121	—
Swansea	a	2011	—	—	2040	—	2137m	2137	—

		FX IC⊘	FO IC⊘	FO IC⊘	FX IC⊘	FO IC	IC⊘	IC⊘	IC⊘
London Paddington	d	1815	1815	1845	1845	1847	1815	1900	1913
Slough	d	—	—	1826	1826	—	1845	1926	1946
Gatwick Airport	d	—	—	1726	1726	—	—	—	1826
Heathrow Airport	d	—	—	1725	1725	—	1755	1825	1855
Reading	d	—	—	1910u	1910	1918	1939	1959	2025
Didcot Parkway	d	1858	1905	1921u	1921	1933	—	—	2010
Swindon	a	1921	1929	1941	1941	1958	2006	2030	2052
Chippenham	a	1934	1945	—	—	2014	—	2043	—
Bath Spa	a	1945	2000	—	—	2027	—	2054	—
Bristol Parkway	a	—	—	2005	2005	—	2030	—	2116
Bristol Temple Meads	a	2000	2015	—	2043	—	—	2109	—
Weston-super-Mare	a	2038	2053	—	—	—	—	2139	—
Newport	a	—	—	2028	2028	—	2052	—	2139
Hereford	a	—	—	—	—	—	2157	—	—
Cardiff Central	a	—	—	2045	2045	—	2108	—	2155
Bridgend	a	—	—	—	—	—	2129	—	2217
Port Talbot Parkway	a	—	—	—	—	—	2141	—	2229
Neath	a	—	—	—	—	—	2148	—	2236
Swansea	a	—	—	—	—	—	2201	—	2249

Notes (London *to* Avon and South Wales pages 2–10)

A	To Milford Haven.
B	22 October, 18 February, 18 March and 29 April only. Also runs to Cardiff on 24 December and 25 March only.
C	22 October, 24 December, 18 February and 18 March only.
D	Until 31 December.
E	From 7 January.
F	Does not run 26 March and 30 April.
G	19 to 23 December, also 23 and 24 March.
a	Arrival time.
b	Bus connection.
c	Until 31 December arrive 2320 by bus.
d	Departure time.
e	By bus from Bath.
g	Change at Bristol Parkway.
h	By bus from Patchway.
k	Change at Redhill and Reading.
m	Tuesday 25 October, Wednesdays 26 October and 22 March, Thursday 27 October and 23 March only.
s	Set down only.
u	Pick up only.
⊘	Buffet service of hot food, sandwiches, hot and cold drinks.
✕	Full meal service plus additional buffet service of hot food, sandwiches, hot and cold drinks.
IC	InterCity service. Catering and seat reservations available. Conveys First and Standard Class accommodation.
P	InterCity Pullman (except Bank Holidays) with full meal service to First Class ticket holders in designated seats. Buffet service of hot food, sandwiches, hot and cold drinks available to all passengers.
}	Runs on certain dates only.
FO	Fridays only.
FX	Fridays excepted.

All trains are reservable except where indicated (†).

> Through trains are shown in **bold** type: connecting services in light type. Connections shown are an indication of journey possibilities and are not guaranteed.

Swansea—Cardiff—Bristol—Bath—London

MONDAYS TO FRIDAYS

		IC	IC⊘	BHX IC⊘	BHX IC⊘	MO IC⊘	MX IC⊘	IC⊘	BHX IC✗
Swansea	d	—	0350	—	—	—	—	—	—
Neath	d	—	0400	—	—	—	—	—	—
Port Talbot Parkway	d	—	0407	—	—	—	—	—	—
Bridgend	d	—	0417	—	—	—	—	—	—
Cardiff Central	d	0439	—	—	0544	—	—	0614	—
Hereford	d	—	0351	—	—	—	—	—	—
Newport	d	—	0453	—	0556	—	—	0626	—
Weston-super-Mare	d	—	—	—	—	0554	—	—	—
Bristol Temple Meads	d	0410	—	0552	—	0622	0622	—	0646
Bristol Parkway	d	—	0519	—	0618	—	—	0648	—
Bath Spa	d	0428	—	0604	—	0634	0634	—	0658
Chippenham	d	—	—	0615	—	0645	0645	—	0709
Swindon	d	0504	0546	0630	0645	0700	0700	0715	0724
Didcot Parkway	a	—	—	0647	0702	0717	0717	—	—
Reading	a	0541	0612	0702	0716	0731	0731	0741	0750
Heathrow Airport	a	0720	0750	—	0850	—	—	—	0920
Gatwick Airport	a	0723	0826	0919	—	—	—	—	—
Slough	a	0635	0705	0732	—	—	—	0825	—
London Paddington	a	0627	0640	0731	0744	0800	0800	0809	0820

		IC✗	IC⊘	IC⊘	A IC✗	IC P	IC⊘	IC✗	IC⊘
Swansea	d	—	0553	—	—	0637	—	—	0709
Neath	d	—	0603	—	—	0647	—	—	0719
Port Talbot Parkway	d	—	0611	—	—	0655	—	—	0726
Bridgend	d	—	0621	—	—	0705	—	—	0736
Cardiff Central	d	—	0642	—	—	0726	—	—	0757
Hereford	d	—	—	—	—	0640	—	—	—
Newport	d	—	0656	—	—	0740	—	—	0811
Weston-super-Mare	d	0628	—	0655	—	—	—	0735	—
Bristol Temple Meads	d	0656	—	0722	0740	—	—	0807	—
Bristol Parkway	d	—	0718	—	0748	0802	—	—	0833
Bath Spa	d	0708	—	0734	—	—	—	0819	—
Chippenham	d	—	—	0745	—	—	—	0830	—
Swindon	d	0730	0745	0800	0815	—	0830	0845	0900
Didcot Parkway	a	—	—	—	—	0847	—	—	—
Reading	a	0801	0817	—	—	—	0901	0911	0926
Heathrow Airport	a	—	—	0950	—	—	—	—	1050
Gatwick Airport	a	—	1008	—	—	—	—	—	1108
Slough	a	0838	0905	—	—	—	—	0947	1005
London Paddington	a	0830	0846	0850	0904	0913	0929	0939	0954

		B IC✗	IC⊘	IC⊘	IC⊘	IC⊘	IC⊘	IC✗	C IC
Swansea	d	0741	—	—	0841	—	—	—	0910
Neath	d	0751	—	—	0851	—	—	—	0922
Port Talbot Parkway	d	0758	—	—	0858	—	—	—	0930
Bridgend	d	0809	—	—	0909	—	—	—	0946
Cardiff Central	d	0830	—	—	0930	0935	—	—	1010
Hereford	d	0730	—	—	—	0839	—	—	—
Newport	d	0844	—	—	0947	—	—	—	1025
Weston-super-Mare	d	—	—	0838	—	—	0920	1003	—
Bristol Temple Meads	d	—	—	0920	—	—	1020	1040	—
Bristol Parkway	d	0906	—	—	1009	—	—	—	—
Bath Spa	d	—	—	0934	—	—	1032	1052	—
Chippenham	d	—	—	0945	—	—	1043	—	—
Swindon	d	—	0931	1000	—	1036	1058	—	—
Didcot Parkway	a	—	0948	—	—	—	1115	—	—
Reading	a	0953	1001	1026	1048	1102	1128	1135	1148
Heathrow Airport	a	1120	—	1150	1220	—	1250	—	—
Gatwick Airport	a	—	—	1208	—	—	1308	—	—
Slough	a	—	1036	1104	—	1136	—	1142	—
London Paddington	a	1021	1029	1054	1116	1130	1200	1204	1222

Fig. 8.2 b) InterCity South Wales–London; Guide to Services

Swansea—Cardiff—Bristol—Bath—London

MONDAYS TO FRIDAYS—*continued*

		ℝ D IC⊘	IC✗	IC⊘	FO IC⊘	IC✗	IC✗	IC⊘	IC✗
Swansea	d	0941	—	1025	—	—	1141	—	1241
Neath	d	0951	—	1037	—	—	1151	—	1251
Port Talbot Parkway	d	0958	—	1045	—	—	1158	—	1258
Bridgend	d	1009	—	1059	—	—	1209	—	1309
Cardiff Central	d	1030	—	1138	—	—	1230	—	1330
Hereford	d	0947	—	1035	—	—	1137	—	1216
Newport	d	1044	—	1144	—	—	1244	—	1344
Weston-super-Mare	d	—	1118	—	—	1203	—	1258	—
Bristol Temple Meads	d	—	1140	—	1225	1240	—	1340	—
Bristol Parkway	d	1106	—	1206	—	—	1306	—	1406
Bath Spa	d	—	1152	—	—	1252	—	1352	—
Chippenham	d	—	1203	—	—	1303	—	1403	—
Swindon	d	1132	1218	1233	—	1318	1333	1418	1433
Didcot Parkway	a	—	1235	—	—	1335	—	1435	—
Reading	a	1158	1248	1257	1318	1348	1359	1448	1458
Heathrow Airport	a	1320	—	1420	1450	—	1520	—	1620
Gatwick Airport	a	1408	—	1508	1508	—	1612	—	1708
Slough	a	1236	—	1311	—	1402	1436	1502	1536
London Paddington	a	1226	1316	1329	1347	1420	1428	1520	1526

		IC✗	IC⊘	IC⊘	IC P	IC⊘	IC⊘	IC✗	IC⊘
Swansea	d	—	1341	—	—	1441	—	—	—
Neath	d	—	1351	—	—	1451	—	—	—
Port Talbot Parkway	d	—	1358	—	—	1458	—	—	—
Bridgend	d	—	1409	—	—	1509	—	—	—
Cardiff Central	d	—	1430	—	—	1530	—	—	—
Hereford	d	—	1341	—	—	1435	—	—	—
Newport	d	—	1444	—	—	1544	—	—	—
Weston-super-Mare	d	1357	—	—	—	—	1543	—	—
Bristol Temple Meads	d	1440	—	1545	—	1605	1623	1640	—
Bristol Parkway	d	—	1506	—	1606	—	1630	—	—
Bath Spa	d	1452	—	1557	—	1617	—	1652	—
Chippenham	d	1503	—	—	—	1628	—	1703	—
Swindon	d	1518	1533	1600	1633	1643	—	1718	—
Didcot Parkway	a	1535	—	1617	—	1700	—	1735	—
Reading	a	1548	1559	1630	—	1659	1713	1718	1748
Heathrow Airport	a	—	1720	1750	—	1820	—	1850	—
Gatwick Airport	a	—	1843	—	—	—	—	—	—
Slough	a	1602	1636	1725	—	—	1727	1805	—
London Paddington	a	1620	1627	1658	1703	1727	1745	1748	1816

		FO IC⊘	IC⊘	IC⊘	IC⊘	IC⊘	IC⊘	IC⊘	IC⊘
Swansea	d	—	1541	—	1641	—	1741	—	1841
Neath	d	—	1551	—	1651	—	1751	—	1851
Port Talbot Parkway	d	—	1558	—	1658	—	1758	—	1858
Bridgend	d	—	1609	—	1709	—	1809	—	1909
Cardiff Central	d	—	1630	—	1730	—	1830	—	1930
Hereford	d	—	1543	—	1640	—	1739	—	1839
Newport	d	—	1644	—	1744	—	1846	—	1944
Weston-super-Mare	d	—	1652	1713e	1720	—	1848	—	—
Bristol Temple Meads	d	1652	—	1730	—	1810	—	1925	—
Bristol Parkway	d	—	1706	—	1806	—	1906	—	2006
Bath Spa	d	1704	—	1742	—	1822	—	1937	—
Chippenham	d	—	—	1753	—	1833	—	1948	—
Swindon	d	1726	1733	1808	1833	1848	1933	2003	2033
Didcot Parkway	a	—	—	1825	—	1905	—	2020	2050
Reading	a	1759	1838	—	1918	1959	2033	—	2103
Heathrow Airport	a	—	1920	2020	2050	2120	—	—	2250
Gatwick Airport	a	—	1953	2108	—	—	2208	—	2312
Slough	a	1813	1915	—	1932	2036	—	—	2136
London Paddington	a	1820	1831	1906	1921	1950	2029	2103	2132

Notes (South Wales and Avon *to* London pages 12–20)

A Full meal service available to First Class ticket holders only.
B Starts at Milford Haven on Mondays.
C All Mondays
Tuesdays 25 October, 3 November, 21, 28 March and 2 May 1989.
Wednesdays 26 October, 28 December, 4 January, 22 and 29 March 1989.
Thursdays 27 October, 22, 29 December, 23 and 30 March 1989.
Fridays 23 and 30 December.
D From Milford Haven.
E 22 October, 11 and 18 February, 18 March, 1 and 8 April only.

a Arrival time.
b Bus connection.
d Departure time.
e Change at Bristol Parkway.
f Change at Swindon.
g Change at Reading and Redhill.
h By bus to Patchway.
s Set down only.

⊘ Buffet service of hot food, sandwiches, hot and cold drinks.
✗ Full meal service plus additional buffet service of hot food, sandwiches, hot and cold drinks.
IC InterCity service. Catering and seat reservations available. Conveys First and Standard Class accommodation.
P InterCity Pullman (except Bank Holidays) with full meal service to First Class ticket holders in designated seats. Buffet service of hot food, sandwiches, hot and cold drinks available to all passengers.
ℝ This train is expected to be very busy and seat reservations are therefore essential. Seat reservations are free on this train.
† Seat reservations are not available on this service.
} Runs on certain dates only.
BHX Does not run on Bank Holidays.
FO Fridays only.
MO Mondays only.
MX Mondays excepted.

> Through trains are shown in **bold** type: connecting services in light type. Connections shown are an indication of journey possibilities and are not guaranteed.

The British Railways Board accepts no liability for any inaccuracy in these tables which may be altered or cancelled at short notice, particularly during public holiday periods. Special timetables will be produced for Christmas and Easter holiday services.

a) Use the extract from the Intercity London to South Wales Guide to Services (Fig 8.2 a)) to look up the time of the most suitable train for Mr Morris to catch from London to Cardiff Central, so that he arrives in time for the meeting at 12.00 noon.

b) Look up the times of trains for the return journey (fig. 8.2b)) and find the latest one he could catch, which would still bring him back to London by 7.00 pm.

COMMENTS ON THE RESEARCHING QUESTION

a) London (Paddington) to Cardiff (Central)

The 1000 from Paddington arriving at Cardiff at 1153 would bring Mr Morris in a little late for the meeting. To arrive in time, he would have to take the 0900 arriving at 1047. Note that the 0930 arriving at 1110, runs only on special days.

b) Cardiff (Central) to London (Paddington)

As the meeting is expected to take approximately 3½ hours, ending at about 3.30 pm (1530 hours), Mr Morris would have to wait for the 1630 from Cardiff, arriving in Paddington at 1831.

It is evident that the trains do not fit in very well with the meeting starting at 12.00 noon and Mr Morris's commitment to be back in London by 7.00 pm. If you were asked to arrange a time to suit Mr Morris, when would you fix the meeting?

TYPING THE ITINERARY

The details of an itinerary should be set out briefly but clearly, using the 24 hour system. Figure 8.3 is an example of a well-presented itinerary containing all the points which an assessor would be looking for.

Overall dates of journey

Name of the person or persons for whom it is intended

```
ITINERARY FOR MR E JOHNSON

8 March to 10 March 19XX

Wednesday 8 March

1445 hrs   Depart London office
           (Taken by company car)

1530       Check-in London (Heathrow)
              Terminal 4
              Flight No 326

1630       Depart London (Heathrow)

1830       Arrive Barcelona Airport
           (To be met by Senor Gonzales)

           Accommodation booked at
              El Cid Hotel
              Ave de los Angeles, 132
              (Single room with bath)

2000       Presentation at El Cid Hotel
              followed by Dinner


Thursday 9 March

1000 hrs   Meeting with directors of
              Soldumar Construction SA,
              Edificio El Rey,
              Ave Grande, 113
              Barcelona

           Tour of site

1730       Depart for Barcelona Airport
           (Taken by Senor Gonzales)

1815       Check-in Barcelona Airport
              Flight 328

1915       Depart Barcelona

1830       Arrive London Heathrow
           (To be met by company car)
```

Day and date
Times using 24-hour clock

Details for the outward journey:
– name of station/airport terminal
– details of reservation
– times for checking in (airport/car ferry)
– time of departure
– time and place of arrival

Details of accommodation

Details of engagements

Details of return journey

Fig 8.3 Example of an itinerary

C O U R S E W O R K   A S S I G N M E N T S

MEG COURSEWORK
EXAMPLE

Situation

You are Assistant Secretary in the Personnel Department of MEG Enterprises. The Personnel Officer, Ms Fiona White has asked you to act on her behalf as she is at a meeting.

TASK 1

Ms White is to travel to London next Wednesday to attend a meeting at Head Office. She asks you to find out the time of a suitable train from the local station, then to type an itinerary incorporating that, plus the following details in logical order:

1300 hours – lunch with Mr J Smithson, 1100 hours – meeting of all Personnel Officers, 1500 hours – tour of offices, Ms White must return by 2000 hours so include the time of a return train in your itinerary.

LEAG ASSIGNMENT
B: SECRETARIAL
TASKS

The next task was set by LEAG in the second coursework assignment and should be carried out in the fifth term of a two-year course. You would be expected to take about 15 to 20 minutes to complete the task.
You work as Secretary to Mr B Copley of J Copley & Co

TASK 2

Mr Copley will travel from his home in Dunstable to Nottingham by car. Refer to the AA Guide and find out the nearest suitable motorway, the junction he will join and his junction exit point for Nottingham. He would also like to know the approximate mileage. Give him the information in the form of a memo.   (*20 marks*)

SEG COURSEWORK
ASSIGNMENT

The following tasks have been taken from a specimen assignment issued by the Southern Examining Group.

You are the Receptionist/Secretary for the Hotel Rober, near Ambleside in the Lake District. The owner of the Hotel, J Robertson, has left a memorandum for you to deal with first thing Monday morning. Your first task is to type up the memorandum correctly and then to deal with the numbered instructions contained in it. Present each part of your work in typewritten form.

TASK 3

Prepare a brief itinerary of places (within 1 hour's drive) to visit in the area for Tuesday, Wednesday and Thursday. Don't forget to include time of departure and approximate return times.

O U T L I N E   A N S W E R S   T O   T A S K S   1 – 3

MEG COURSEWORK
EXAMPLE

TASK 1: FINDING TRAIN TIMES AND PREPARING AN ITINERARY

Remember to include the standard items found in an itinerary, including a title to indicate who the itinerary is for and the date of the journey.

When looking up the times of the trains, you should allow Ms White sufficient time to get to the meeting at 1000 in the morning, and find a train which gets her back by 2000.

TASK 2: PLANNING A CAR JOURNEY

You are advised to use an AA Guide to plan the journey. If you are not sure where Dunstable and Nottingham are, start by looking them up in the AA Gazetteer for England, which lists the main towns and cities and their map references in the AA Atlas. You will be able to identify from the AA Atlas the nearest motorway linking them together, and can then refer to the detailed motorway map, for the appropriate motorway junction entry and exist numbers.

To calculate the distance from Dusntable to Nottingham, you will need to refer to the AA motorway map for the mileage from each centre to the motorway, and add this to the total distance between the two junctions.

Make sure you present your answer in the form of a *memo*.

> 66 When working out mileage over a distance, jot the figures down and use a calculator to check your total. 99

SEG COURSEWORK ASSIGNMENT

TASK 3: PREPARING AN ITINERARY OF PLACES OF INTEREST TO VISIT

The AA Guide would probably be the most useful book to help you plan the itinerary. Try to find three places to visit that are in different directions. Remember that they should be about 1 hour's drive – approximately 40 miles – from Ambleside or whatever the starting point you are using.

A STUDENT'S ANSWER TO TASK 2 AND EXAMINER COMMENTS

LEAG ASSIGNMENT B: SECRETARIAL TASKS

TASK 2: PLANNING A CAR JOURNEY USING AN AA GUIDE

> 66 The heading M E M O R A N D U M was omitted, otherwise full marks for the layout. 99

```
To:      Mr Copley                    Date: 25 March 1988

From:    Alison Baker                 Ref:  JC/ab

JOURNEY FROM DUNSTABLE TO NOTTINGHAM

The information you asked for is as follows:

The nearest suitable motorway from Dunstable to Nottingham is
the M 1 motorway.  You can join it at junction 11.  The exit
for Nottingham is Exit 25.

The total distance is approximately 89 miles.

If you need any more information please let me know.
```

> 66 The details are correct, except for the distance from Dunstable to Nottingham. The figure given is the mileage for the motorway only. 99

A TUTOR'S ANSWER TO TASK 1

MEG COURSEWORK EXAMPLE

TASK 1: FINDING TRAIN TIMES AND PREPARING AN ITINERARY

ITINERARY

Ms Fiona White - Meeting at Head Office London

Wednesday 22 February 1990

0926	Depart Reading station
0954	Arrive London (Paddington)
1100	Meeting of all personnel officers
1300	Lunch with Mr J Smithson
1500	Tour of offices
1915	Depart London (Paddington)
1939	Arrive Reading station

GETTING STARTED

Audio-typing is simply typing from sound which is in the form of recorded dictation. There are several advantages to both the employer and the typist in using this form of dictation rather than shorthand.

Most importantly, it is time-saving. When an employer dictates to a secretary who writes shorthand, it means *both* people have to be present at the *same time*. With audio dictation, the employer can dictate when convenient; this might be at home or even on the way to the office. The secretary can be getting on with other work whilst dictation is taking place.

Transcription can be done in the typist's own time and at her own speed. Where there are difficulties interpreting the work, the recording can be played over and over again.

All typists appreciate the necessity to check their work thoroughly. In the case of audio-typing, this can easily be done by playing back the recording.

Audio-typing is not new. Offices have been using this form of dictation and transcription for many years. It is obvious then that the examining bodies will want to test this skill. In the GCSE, Audio-transcription forms an integral part of the LEAG Office Technology and Communications examination and an option in the SEG Keyboarding Applications examinations where the Audio-transcription element is the same as the Royal Society of Arts examinations of that name at Stages I or II.

ESSENTIAL PRINCIPLES

Key words
Here are a few words which need watching. Because they sound similar and because of poor dictation they may be incorrectly produced if you are unaware of the spelling and meanings. Check their meanings with a dictionary and then learn the correct spelling.

accept/except	eminent/imminent
access/excess	enable/unable
addition/edition	enforce/in force
affect/effect	faint/feint
ascent/assent	finally/finely
advice/advise	formally/formerly
assistance/assistants	loose/lose
assure/ensure/insure/unsure	personal/personnel
board/bored	piece/peace
check/cheque	practise/practice
companies/company's	residence/residents
compliment/complement	site/sight
correspondence/correspondents	stationary/stationery
decease/disease	to/too/two
device/devise	whose/who's
elicit/illicit	your/you're

Note also words which MUST be written separately

thank you
every day   BUT everything
per cent   BUT percentage

AND words which should contain a hyphen

by-law
co-operate/co-operation/co-operative
part-time
time-table
up-to-date

Audio-typing is a *combination* of skills. Firstly you must be an expert typist who knows the rules of display. Secondly you need to be able to spell reasonably well and have a good knowledge of punctuation. Although it is possible to stop the recording in order to look up difficult words in a dictionary, this can be very time-consuming and causes lack of concentration. Familiarity with words which sound similar but have different meanings is important. A list of some of these can be found in the chart of Key Words.

Take care with instructions which may be given in more than one manner. Some people refer to a *solidus* sign, others call it the *oblique*.

Brackets are often referred to as *parentheses* and *full stops* as *periods*.

Listen carefully for instructions to use 'block capitals' or to open or close quotes – this means use double not single quotes.

Consistency is still important

As a good touch-typist you will be used to keeping your eyes on the copy. With audio-typing there is no copy. It is quite acceptable to keep your eyes on what is being typed – on the paper, or on the VDU if word processing. Don't be tempted to start looking at the keys. Touch-typing is just as important for the audio-typist if speed and accuracy is to be achieved.

The object of audio-training is to be able to type continuously whilst listening to the dictation. However, this requires a fast typing speed, since most dictators speak at well over 60 words per minute (wpm). For this reason, most typists listen to a few words, stop the tape and then type those words from memory. Before long you find you can start listening to the next few words before you have quite finished typing the last words so you achieve continuous typing without actually keeping up to the speed of the dictator.

To build up this skill, it is wise to begin with listening to only *two* or *three* words, stopping the tape and typing those words before listening to the next two or three words and so on. Gradually, you begin to listen to quite long phrases or short sentences and eventually you listen to a whole sentence before typing it.

Obviously you must be a good listener and not mind being locked in your 'own little world' whilst concentrating on the sounds coming through the headphones. Most dictators will be considerate enough to give you essential information at the beginning of the tape, information such as:

a) The type of document – usually memo or letter – and the stationery to be used.
b) How many copies are required.
c) The approximate length of the document – although this can be assessed from the actual equipment in some cases.
d) Special instructions such as marking the document 'Confidential'.

There may also be a set of written notes or other documents referred to provided with the tape. This is certainly the case in most examinations. Considerate dictators will also spell out unfamiliar words for you, particularly names.

3 > EQUIPMENT

Within the office situation this can vary greatly. Larger firms will have a sophisticated, centralized system, probably linked to the internal telephone system and the typing pool. Here the dictation may be recorded on discs, belts or tapes. In training and during the examination you will probably use a desk-top model which resembles a tape recorder. Dictation is made onto a tape cassette which is inserted into the *transcriber*. The typist listens through headphones and controls the machine with a foot control which allows her to play, stop, re-wind and replay.

Some transcribers show the *length* of each document and the amount of space taken up with dictation so far or space still available on the tape.

As with word processing or typewriting, it is essential that you are familiar with your equipment well before the examination.

EXAMINATION QUESTIONS

Remember to check your work and correct all errors before taking it from the machine

Examiners of audio-typing will be looking for basically the same skills as in a typewriting examination – well-displayed, accurately typed work completed within the requisite time. The length of time allowed will vary with the different examinations.

As with typewriting and word processing examinations, you will be expected to show that you are capable of reading, understanding and following instructions. These may be given on the tape recording or be written on a separate sheet.

When typing letters and memos you can expect to have to take *carbon copies* and type *envelopes*. Form filling may be tested, with the information to be typed given on the recording. Most audio-typing examinations include some exercises to be typed from written drafts, usually manuscript. Questions involving display, tabulation or various documents, such as minutes and agendas, come within this category.
Let us now look at some past GCSE questions.

AUDIO-TYPING LETTERS

Question 1

AUDIO INSTRUCTION (TO BE DICTATED)

Please key-in and print the following standard letter leaving space at the points identified for the insertion of details at a later date.

You'll need to leave top, left and right hand margins of no more than 25mm or the letter won't fit on one side of A4.

'Dear (leave a blank space)

We are pleased to offer you employment as (leave a blank space) in our (leave a blank space) Division. (new paragraph)

Initially you will be based at our Stevenage Office, with a total salary of (leave a blank space). At some later date, it may be necessary for you to move to our London office and this would entitle you to an additional (leave a blank space) Outer London Allowance. This will be paid monthly into your bank account on the last working day of each calendar month.

You will be provided with a company car and a letter containing the rules and conditions of the Company Scheme is enclosed along with our current car list. It is company policy that a new car is only ordered when there is no suitable unused car within the company. This offer of employment is made on the understanding that you are in possession of a full valid driving licence and continued employment in this position is conditional upon your maintaining your licence. (new paragraph)

In order to accept this offer, please sign one copy of this letter, complete the names and addresses of references in the space provided and return it to me within seven days. Should you require any further information please do not hesitate to contact me.

Yours sincerely

Peter Parsons
Personnel Manager (end of dictation)

Would you please add the section on references, which I've put in your tray, to the end of this letter please. (end of task)

I would like to accept this offer and agree to the company taking up my references. I will be able to commence employment on:

Date   ....

Signed ....   Date ....

Reference   *Reference*
....

....

....

ADVICE AND COMMENTS

Most of the information you have to type will be recorded for you. The dictator will have warned you about the size of margins thereby indicating the length of the task.

You are obviously producing a standard (form) letter in which you have to leave *blank spaces* at certain points. You must decide how much *space* to leave. Imagine the kind of information which may have to be inserted later and be generous. For example, on the first line of the first paragraph you have to leave sufficient space to insert a type of employment. Imagine you may later have to insert "Area Sales Representative". You will need to leave at least 24 letters plus the space before and after the insertion. Yet, later in the passage, where salary is to be inserted, much less space will be required.

Notice also that this task incorporates other data not supplied on the recording but given on the accompanying question paper.

FORM FILLING

Question 2
Please type in the details on the attached form. My middle initial is N. Put my home address – 14 Roundhay Avenue, Darlington, Co Durham. I have been playing golf for 12 years and my current handicap is 15. I am currently a member of Fordbridge Golf Club. My proposer is Mr. T. Kenton and my seconder is Mr. J. Curtess. I shall enclose a cheque for £200. Leave the form undated.

Moorpark Golf Club

Parkside, Sunderland, Co Durham   Telephone Sunderland 69547

APPLICATION FOR MEMBERSHIP

NAME _____

ADDRESS _____

_____

TEL NO (Home) _____   _____ (Business) _____

PREVIOUS GOLFING EXPERIENCE _____

OTHER GOLF CLUBS _____

_____

CURRENT HANDICAP _____

PROPOSED BY _____

SECONDED BY _____

MEMBERSHIP FEES

FULL MEMBER £150.00 ☐   NEW MEMBER £20.00 ☐

COUNTRY MEMBER £50.00 ☐   JUNIOR MEMBER £50.00 ☐

Please put an X in the box opposite the category of membership for which
you are applying.

I enclose Cheque/Cash for £ _____
(Please delete as necessary)

SIGNED: _____ DATE: _____

Please return the completed form together with your remittance to:

Mr Peter Laird, Secretary, Moorpark Golf Club
You are reminded that your application will go before the General
Committee for approval. You will be notified in writing of the Committee's
decision.

TUTOR'S ANSWER TO QUESTION 2

Moorpark Golf Club

Parkside, Sunderland, Co Durham   Telephone Sunderland 69547

APPLICATION FOR MEMBERSHIP

NAME   Paul N Daly

ADDRESS   14 Roundhay Avenue

             Darlington, Co Durham

TEL NO (Home) _____ (Business) _____

PREVIOUS GOLFING EXPERIENCE   Player for past 12 years

OTHER GOLF CLUBS   Fordbridge Golf Club

CURRENT HANDICAP   15

PROPOSED BY   Mr T Kenton

SECONDED BY   Mr J Curtess

MEMBERSHIP FEES

FULL MEMBER £150.00 ☐   NEW MEMBER £20.00 ☐

COUNTRY MEMBER £50.00 ☐   JUNIOR MEMBER £50.00 ☐

Please put an X in the box opposite the category of membership for which you are applying.

I enclose Cheque/Cash for £ 200.00
(Please delete as necessary)

SIGNED: _____ DATE: _____

Please return the completed form together with your remittance to:

Mr Peter Laird, Secretary, Moorpark Golf Club
You are reminded that your application will go before the General Committee for approval. You will be notified in writing of the Committee's decision.

MEMORANDA

Question 3

Type the following A5 memorandum to the Managing Director from me (Paul Daly). I will sign it tomorrow.

I have written to Mr A Sonzogni confirming the arrangements for the Antiques Fair which is to be held here on 22nd June.

As a large number of visitors is anticipated, I am arranging for an additional buffet lunch to be available between noon and 2 pm. I shall engage any necessary extra staff to assist in the preparation and serving of such a lunch.

ADVICE AND COMMENTS

This examination question was not taken from an actual examination paper but is quite representative. The introductory page of the question paper would have included some extra information, such as the following::

'You are Personal Secretary to Mr Paul Daly, Manager of the Tudor Palace Hotel, Newcastle Upon Tyne. Mr. Daly has asked you to type the following tasks:'

You will notice that some of this information is required to assist you in completing the form.

Although there is no home telephone number given for Mr Daly, his business telephone number may have been available if printed headed paper was supplied for use with another task.

A STUDENT'S ANSWER TO QUESTION 3

```
                        M E M O R A N D U M


        TO    Managing Director

        FROM  Paul Daly                        1 June 1989

        I have written to Mr A Sonzogni confirming the arrangments for the
        Antiques fair which is to be held here on 22nd June.

        As a large number of visiters are anticipated, I am arranging for an
        additional buffet lunch to be available between noon and 2pm.  I shall
        engage any necessary extra staff to assist in the preperation and
        serving of such a lunch.
```

Open punctuation

Spelling!

COMMENTS

Although not taken from an actual examination paper this is typical of an audio typing question. The information may have been produced in typewritten form, as in this case, or in manuscript. Alternatively it could have been recorded on tape.

It is hoped that the candidate used *tomorrow's* date, as instructed.

As usual, this appears to be a correctly typed and well-displayed piece of work. A closer scrutiny, however, reveals some quite serious errors. In the office situation this would not be a 'mailable' copy.

There are a number of spelling errors. Where a typist is not sure of the correct spelling, time must be reserved for checking with a dictionary.

USEFUL FOLLOW-UP WORK

We have taken four questions from past examinations set by SEG to give you some extra practice on this topic.

TASK 1

This question has been taken from SEG Keyboarding Applications – Winter Series 1988 Audio Typewriting Paper 2A – General Level. The following will be dictated on to appropriate equipment at a speed of approximately 70 wpm, prior to the examination. At the time of the examination you will be required to type this from the recorded dictation. Notice how the dictator helps you by giving specific instructions and spelling out difficult words.

For pre-recording:

'Task One

MEMORANDUM OF 97 WORDS

Type the following A4 memo to all Staff from the Personnel Manager. Date for today.

The (initial capitals) Annual Company Outing will this year be a full (hyphen) day trip to London. (paragraph)

Transport, which will be by (initial capital) Redline coach, will be provided at the (initial capital) Company's expense, and depart from the main office block. (paragraph)

It is expected that arrival in (initial capitals) Trafalgar (T – R – A – F – A – L – G – A – R) Square will be by ten thirty hours, and staff will then be free to enjoy the remainder of the day. (full stop) An evening meal will be provided at the (initial capitals) Cowood (C – O – W – O – O – D) Hotel on the journey home and an outline menu is attached. (paragraph)

All staff and their families are invited and a list of places of interest is enclosed. (fullstop)

End of Task One.'

TASK 2

The following instructions will be recorded on tape. You will notice there are also instructions on the manuscript draft provided.

'Task Two

Type a copy of the list of places of interest for inclusion with my memorandum to Staff.

End of Instructions for Task Two'

ELITE GROUP

OUTING TO LONDON
Saturday 27 May 1989

PLACES OF INTEREST

Museum of London – London Wall
Exhibits include Lord Mayor's Coach and Great Fire of London Room. Stations – Barbican and St Pauls

Covent Garden
Market Hall restored and now opened as shops, studios, cafes and promenades. Station – Covent Garden

Telecom Tower
Tallest in London – 620 ft high. Stations – Warren Street/Goodge Street

Barbican Centre
Theatre, Library, Art Gallery, Cinemas, roof top conservatory and restaurants. Station – Barbican

London Transport Museum – Covent Garden
Historic vehicles including horse busses, motor buses, trams and trolley buses. Station – Covent Garden

Art Galleries
National Gallery, Trafalgar Square   Station – Trafalgar Square
National Portrait, St Martin's Place, WC2   Station – Charing Cross
Tate Gallery, Millbank, SW1   Station – Pimlico

ENJOY YOUR DAY!

Rejoin Redline Coach, Trafalgar Square at 1830 hrs *promptly* please.

Tasks 3 and 4 are again from the SEG Keyboarding Applications Winter 1988 examination but this time from the Audio Typing Extended Level – Paper 2B.

TASK 3

The following will be pre-recorded:

'A LETTER OF 196 WORDS

Type a letter on A4 headed paper with a carbon copy. The letter should be marked Private and Confidential and is to Mr A V Wilson. Mark the carbon copy For the attention of Mr John Jones.

Dear Mr Wilson (HEADING FOLLOWS – IN CAPS PLEASE)

POLICIES HELD WITH NEWTON INSURANCE GROUP

With further reference to the above and our recent acquisition of the (initial capital) Group, we now have pleasure in confirming that your policies have been revised in accordance with the instructions contained in your letter. (full stop) Details are given below and should there be any queries, please contact this office without delay. (paragraph)

(Typist – the following paragraphs are to be typed as A and B)

a (Caps and paragraph heading) HOME INSURANCE COVER This policy now covers a total sum insured of (pound sign) twelve thousand with a single article limit of (pound sign) two thousand. (full stop) All high risk items and cover for contents of your freezer are unchanged (dash) premiums remain payable by monthly instalments. (full stop).

b (Caps and paragraph heading) LIFE ASSURANCE COVER (initial capitals) Annual Bonus Rates have recently been declared and we are sure you will be delighted with the value of the enclosed certificate. (full stop) We are proceeding to obtain quotations for further personal life (oblique) mortgage cover and the appropriate (initial capitals) Proposal Form is enclosed for your early completion. (paragraph)

All policies previously held with the (initial capitals) Newton Group have been transferred to the above office and we trust that the merger of the Groups will result in an improved service for all our clients. (paragraph)

We await your reply.

Yours sincerely
ELITE GROUP INSURANCE SERVICES

A THOMAS
District Manager

Type and envelope'

TASK 4

You will be advised, on the recording, to:

'Type a copy of the three column table on A5 paper following all instructions'

POLICIES HELD WITH ELITE GROUP INSURANCE SERVS
MR BRIAN HARRISON

CLASSIFICATION	POLICY NUMBER	COVER
MOTOR (4)	AR 832157P	Jewellery/ Item limit £5,000
HOUSEOWNERS COMPREHENSIVE (3)	A/6551005	£10,000/With Profits
PERSONAL ACCIDENT (5)	HPO 952112	House/contents Abbey Fields
ENDOWMENT (2)	MP 190899	1987 Rover Value £8,000
ALL RISKS – ANN HARRISON (1)	PA 158632	Unlimited

Typist: change to numbered order as shown

G E T T I N G   S T A R T E D

Table 10.1 on page 120 lists the GCSE examinations which include word processing in the syllabuses. As can be seen from the Table, you can choose to do word processing either as an optional paper in one of the typewriting examinations, such as in SEG Keyboarding Applications, or, if you are doing an IT examination, as one of the software applications.

In some of the typewriting examinations the student is allowed to use a word processor *instead* of a typewriter, especially when doing course work. It is believed that eventually, word processors will supersede typewriters in all the typewriting examinations.

Whether you are doing word processing as part of your typing course, or as an option in an IT exam, you will be expected to show that you are able to use the system – this can be either a dedicated word processor or a microcomputer with a word-processing package. Depending on the level of the examination, you will be expected to carry out a number of tasks and produce one or more documents – in the extended levels more advanced functions and wider range of documents are required. The ways that these skills are assessed are summarized in Table 10.1.

Whatever the method of assessment you will be expected to show that you can:

1 Log on and load the system.
2 Create a text file and key in material.
3 Store and save the file for future editing.
4 Recall and alter text which has been keyed in.
5 Use various facilities to manipulate and rearrange text.
6 Print out hard copies of the document.
7 Carry out various file operations such as copying, deleting and renaming.
8 Log off or close down the system.

ESSENTIAL PRINCIPLES

GROUP	EXAMINATION			TIME (HOURS)	MARK	
LEAG	Office Technology & Communications	Paper 1 Machine skills		2	30	5 tasks testing use of typewriter and/or microcomputer/word processor
		Coursework		Total of 12	40	Complete 2 assignments 6 tasks in each, measuring abilities across whole syllabus including data handling with spead-sheet or database
MEG	Office Studies & Information Processing	Paper 2 Practical skills Word processing Database: add or delete data and transfer to another file Spreadsheet: Make calculation and print results		1½	30	3 tasks testing use of either computer/word processor or electronic typewriter with memory, running word processing, databases & spreadsheet packages
		Coursework		Approx 16	27	4 assignments. At least 1 must be produced on computer/word processor or memory typewriter.
NEA	Information Technology Syllabus A					
	Core Module: Data Handling Systems	End of Module Practical Exercise		Not stipulated	30	Select 1 task from choice of 3 using word processing, or database or spreadsheet
		Continuous Assessment of Practical Skills		Not stipulated	30	Assessment of ability to use word processing database and spreadsheet packages
	Extension Module: Electronic Office	Practical Assessment		Not stipulated	60	Assessment of ability to use above packages; also other office software tools
NEA	Information Technology Syllabus B					
	Optional Modules: Application of Word Processing	Continuous Assessment of Practical Skills		Not stipulated		Demonstrate ability to use specific application
	Application of Databases and Spreadsheets	Coursework assignment		Not stipulated		1 assignment to include application of practical skills
SEG	Keyboarding Applications	Option Paper 2 Paper 2A/WP or Paper 2B/WP		2	40	6 word processing tasks
	SEG/RSA Keyboarding Applications (Modular)					
	Module 2 Core Text Processing Skills			1		Candidates may use word processor or typewriter

GROUP EXAMINATION		TIME MARK (HOURS)	
Module 4 Word Processing Stage I		1½	Complete 4 single page business tasks
Module 7 Word Processing Stage II Part 1		1¼	Complete 3 tasks in continuous text (eg report, article)
SEG/RSA Information Technology			
Module 2: CLAIT: Word Processing Spreadsheet Database applications	Coursework Assignments		Assignments set in context of the applications

Table 10.1 GCSE Examinations with word processing options

1 > EDITING TEXT

All the examinations require text to be **entered**, or 'keyed in'. This could either be from typescript with corrections, or from manuscript. In some cases, as in the word processing option paper in SEG Keyboarding Applications and the LEAG Machine Skills paper, the source might be a taped message, or you might be asked to compose a letter or memo based on information given. At the extended level you should expect to prepare a document requiring a tabulated display. The task of inputting text is generally not very well done and marks are lost through:

a) **not following instructions** over **layout**, especially when required to leave a space of certain dimensions in a document
b) **omitting** words or portions of the **text** – each word omitted can incur an accuracy penalty, so if a line of text is left out, the penalities can mount up at an alarming rate
c) **failing** to follow **punctuation** and **capitalisation**
d) **misspelling**; this is one of the more common ways of losing marks. Again, the penalties are high, so it might be worth your while to run a spelling check if you have one.

"Use the special facilities available to speed you up when keying in text"

A few minutes spent reading the instructions and working out the display before you start are never wasted. You can always save precious time when you are keying in, by making full use of the special facilities on a word processer, such as automatic centring, insetting of paragraphs, and so on.

Always allow yourself enough time to check your document before you store it for printing – valuable marks are often wasted through hurried or insufficient screen proof reading.

2 > ENTERING TEXT

In some cases, you are expected to key in and store the text yourself in the first stage, and then recall and **edit** it in the second. In most of the multiple task papers, the text will have been prepared in advance and stored by your teacher, ready for you to recall and edit. The number of functions and the degree of sophistication will depend on the level of the examination you are taking. Practice will give you confidence, so it is important that you know exactly what functions you might be expected to carry out, and the most efficient way of doing them on your system. Below is a typical list of the functions you might expect. It will help you to tackle the editing task, if, in addition to listing any instructions, you always identify and label the functions you have to carry out. Numbering them in the order in which you plan to do them will also help to ensure that you carry them all out. You will find an example of this analysis in the next section in Task 2.

Here are the **main basic editing facilities** you might expect to be asked to do:

Insert a character, word, a string of words and phrases, sentence, paragraph, line space or space within the body of the text
Delete a character, word etc. (as above) within the body of the text
Replace a character or words of the same or different lengths
Move a paragraph from one location to another
Run on two paragraphs
Split a section of text into two paragraphs
Centre a line, or lines of text
Underline a heading or a word in the text or remove the underlining.

EDITING PITFALLS

Here are some of the pitfalls you might encounter when editing:

a) when *deleting a sentence*, or (more often) when *running on two paragraphs*: not leaving sufficient hard spaces after a full stop.
    This happens when deleting the returns – the text closes up to the cursor, which will usually be immediately to the right of the full stop. Just remember to insert *two* hard spaces when you have finished the operation.
b) when *moving a paragraph*: leaving a gap in the place where it was located, or not having a line space between the paragraphs in the new location.
    Use the correct procedure to identify the block you wish to move, making sure you place the cursor on the *first* character of the block and then highlighting or making the whole paragraph, *plus one line space*. When you move the block to the new position, place the cursor on the *first* character of the paragraph which you wish to move down.
c) *failing to underline text* correctly or to *remove underlining*.
    This can be tricky, since most systems will not allow you to cheat and do it manually. The general principle is either to display the command and delete it, or to repeat the command and so cancel the original one – but do make sure you know how to operate your particular system.

3 ⟩ REFORMATTING TEXT

When creating a new document, you will be able to use a ready-made format stored on your system. However, you will have to know how to change the format in the following ways:

Line lengths: shortening or lengthening them.
Insetting: a paragraph from the left margin or from both sides.
Line spacing: changing from single to double, or vice versa.
Line ending: changing from justified to ragged, or vice versa.
Page lengths: shortening or lengthening the page by inserting or removing the page break.

REFORMATTING PITFALLS

The main problems are:

a) *setting margins in the wrong position*: be sure you know the default on your particular system and that you understand the information you are given on the ruler line
b) *failing to follow instructions* with regard to *line spacing, justifying* and so on. With some systems there is no change in the text on the screen when you give these commands, so you would not know just by looking at the screen, whether you have given the correct instructions until printing, when it may be too late. With systems such as these, it is essential that you know how to *display* the print commands. In fact it is a good idea to display the embedded commands whenever changing the format.

4 ⟩ SCREEN PROOF READING

This skill is considered so important that most of the examinations have a specific task which requires proof reading. Text containing a number of deliberate mistakes is keyed in beforehand by the teacher, and the candidate then has to recall the document and proof read it on the screen, checking it against correct copy which might be handwritten or have the errors ringed.

Proof reading is never easy, especially on a screen. Various methods are recommended; possibly the safest is to move the cursor *character by character*, while running your finger along the hard copy. Try to get as much practice as you can, as screen proof reading is fundamental to all the tasks you do.

Look out for errors in *punctuation* and in *spelling*, and for *words omitted* which do not make a noticeable difference to the meaning of the text. These are often the most difficult to identify.

Here is an example of a proof reading task similar to the ones set in the SEG/RSA Keyboarding Applications (Modular) Word Processing production tests, where the passage has to be keyed in, in advance, by the teacher. Even if you are not taking the examination, this type of task will help you to practise proof reading from the screen while checking against a hard copy.

In addition to containing several deliberate mistakes, the text in this test is keyed in with either a ragged or justified right margin and in either single or double line spacing. The candidate is required to *recall* the file containing the document, *correct* the errors which will be circled on the hard copy, and then *print out* with the right margin ragged (if it was previously justified) or vice versa. Similarly, the *line spacing* would have to be altered.

PROOF READING TASK: INSTRUCTIONS TO TUTOR

This task must be keyed in a) with ragged/justified margin and b) in single/double line spacing.
Deliberate errors are marked and must be copied exactly as shown.

If questioned as to why Man wears clothes, most of us would surely answer 'for reasons of warmth and modesty'. However, long before our ancestors put on their first animal furs they decorated their bodies with tattooes and paint()It must follow that this desire for adornment – often indicated by our taste in clothes- says something about our personality, despite what may be considreed stylish at the time. Looking back at period costumes we frequently see fashions recurring and, indeed, old photographs, museums and even jumble sales can provide us with with interesting alternatives to the current trend. In the end the majority of us will dress to suit the occasion, the climate, our mood and budget, which is what makes wradrobes so fascinatingly different!

PROOF READING TASK: INSTRUCTIONS TO THE CANDIDATE

Recall the document. Please amend the circled errors. Then save as (file name) and print out a copy on A4 paper with a justified right margin in single line spacing.
NOTE: In this examination, the candidate is presented with a hard copy of the text with the errors circled, similar to that given to the tutor (see above).

Here are some suggestions on how the corrections could be carried out as quickly as possible, depending on the facilities at your disposal. Try to get into the habit of using the most efficient method of moving the cursor over the text. Remember that this is not always by means of the arrow keys! The numbers refer to the errors in the text.

1 *Delete* character 'e' then cursor to right of 'w' and insert 'e' or *overtype* 'ew' with 'we'
2 *Insert* full stop
3 *Insert* space between 's' and dash
4 As for (1)
5 Use *delete word* facility
6 As for (1)

You will find an example below of a copy which has been corrected and printed out in single line spacing and justified right margin as instructed.

```
If  questioned  as  to  why  Man  wears  clothes,  most  of  us  would
surely  answer  'for  reasons  of  warmth  and  modesty',    However,
long  before  our  ancestors  put  on  their  first  animal  furs  they
decorated  their  bodies  with  tattooes  and  paint,      It  must
follow  that  this  desire  for  adornment  –  often  indicated  by  our
taste  in  clothes  --  says  something  about  our  personality,
despite  what  may  be  considered  stylish  at  the  time,    Looking
back  at  period  costumes  we  frequently  see  fashions  recurring
and,  indeed,  old  photographs,  museums  and  even  jumble  sales
can  provide  us  with  interesting  alternatives  to  the  current
trend,    In  the  end  the  majority  of  us  will  dress  to  suit  the
occasion,  the  climate,  our  mood  and  budget,  which  is  what
makes  wardrobes  so  fascinatingly  different!
```

---

5 > PRINTING OUT   In all the production tests a *hard copy* must be printed out. This is another weak area with many candidates. Poor printing might be due to the limitations of the equipment, but very often it is evidence of lack of practice. If printing out has to be done after the test has been completed, you are not allowed to alter your work once you have reached the printing stage, so careful screen proof reading and a check of printing instructions while you still have access to the document, are both extremely important.

This is sometimes called locate and replace. You might be asked to use this facility in a longer document which has been keyed in previously. It can save a great deal of time, particularly when the word or string of characters can be replaced automatically.

INSERTING VARIABLE INFORMATION

The standard document, usually a letter, has been normally keyed in beforehand and the candidate has to recall and insert the variable information manually. In some cases, the entry point is indicated by a code or symbol – if this is so, you could use the *search facility* to locate the recurring point – or each point is numbered. In either case, remember to check afterwards that you have deleted all the markers and replaced them with the appropriate variable. You should not, of course, alter the layout of the document when doing so.

In some exams, such as paper 2A in the SEG Keyboarding Applications and the Word Processing Module 4 in the SEG/RSA exam, the standard letter has *gaps* instead of markers in it and you are told to enter the information in the appropriate spaces. In this sort of exercise you have to be careful to put the details in the right places and remember to *delete* the extra spaces afterwards.

If you are given a form to complete, great care should be taken not to alter the layout. Switch to overtype if the facility is available.
The basic skills mentioned above appear in all the examinations. The ones listed below feature in the *extended examinations*.

INSERTING STANDARD INFORMATION OR TEXT ('BOILERPLATING')

Here again text, usually a paragraph, is stored in advance of the examination and has to be inserted in the correct position into a document created by the candidate. In some cases, part of the text which you have recalled may have to be *deleted*. If you are asked to do this, read the instructions very carefully again when the text is displayed on the screen.

8 > MAIL MERGING

This is included in the IT syllabuses. It is the preparation of personalised letters to be used in, for example, a mail shot. In most cases a data file containing names and addresses and sometimes other information is prepared and stored in advance. You then have to prepare the standard letter and merge the stored data. You will be dependent to a large extent on how well the database has been tested when it was set up, but you should always check carefully that the entries have merged in the right places before printing out your copy.

Try to bear these points in mind when you are doing the tasks in the next Section. You might also find it useful to take a look again at the hints in Chapter 2 on tackling the typewriting examinations.

EXAMINATION QUESTIONS

In this section you will find a selection of tasks taken from the current GCSE examinations. Some of the more advanced operations, which are on the syllabuses of the extended examinations, have been placed at the end of this section.
Note: Where the document has to be keyed in and stored by the specialist teacher in advance of the exam, try to get someone else to prepare the material for you. If this is not possible, you might find it helpful if you attempted the task some time after you have keyed in the text.

LEAG OTC PAPER 1

TASK 1: TEXT CREATION

In this task you will be able to demonstrate your ability to *open* or *create* a new file, and key in text. Although you can always alter the text afterwards, it will save you time if you make sure beforehand that you have understood *all* the instructions. Take advantage of the hint you are given about the shoulder headings.

Only 1 clear line space here

NOTES
GENERAL / ON CHARTERING

Print a correct version of these notes adding the handwritten section at the end. Check for errors and correct any you find.

We have compiled these notes on chartering following

requests from new clients. We hope they are sufficiently

comprehensive to be of use toseasoned dinghy sailors,

perhaps sailing a yacht for the first time, or similarly to

boat owners, now chartering. we hope they are comprehensive

but your comments would be gratefully appreciated.

Print in single line spacing

change headings to below – WHAT TO BRING

→ TAKEOVER   the charterer should note where all gear, etc is
stowed on board. Particular attention should be paid to
instructions given during demnstration on the use of all
electrical, gas and mechanical equipment.

→ FATIGUE   Many crews arrive for takeover after a long
~~distance~~ drive. It is a great mistake to get under way
without having a meal and a good rest. Without these
fatigue may set in and this will affect your judgement,
efficiency and the safety of the crew and yacht.

SEASICKNESS   Try to avoid anti-histamine tablets; they tend
to make you sleepy. The best tablets are Kwells, Stugeron
or Maxalon. Avoid fatty foods for a week before sailing.
Take aerated drinks with you but no alcohol. eat dry
biscuits at frequent ∧ and suck glucose sweets. If you really   ∧ *intervals*
do suffer badly don't go below but stay in the fresh air and
fix your eyes on a point which is stationary.

WHAT TO BRING
We will provide cooking utensils, crockery, cleaning materials and toilet paper. Freshly laundered sleeping bags are available for hire. You will need to bring:

Indent this section 5 spaces from left margin

at least 2 sets of warm clothing
sensible deck shoes
good quality wet weather gear
food and drink
suntan oil

TASK 2: TEXT AMENDMENT

Both this task and the next one are typical examples of a task where you are asked to recall and amend a document which has been keyed in previously. In both cases, a passage containing a number of deliberate errors has to be keyed in, in advance, by the teacher.

It will be especially useful to get someone else to key in the passage for you, but if you do have to prepare it yourself, try to do so in advance, so that you can let some time elapse before you tackle the candidate's task.

Your screen proof reading and several editing skills are being tested, so it will help you to carry out *all* the amendments successfully, if you list the instructions on the lines suggested below.

Text for Task 2
Instructions to teacher.

The document should be keyed in, prior to the start of the examination. Type the document below laid out in the style shown and save it with a filename of INFHOTEL.

A 50 space typing line must be used.

The circled words should be typed as they appear on the document.

The words 'Candidate number' and 'Candidate name' must be added to either the beginning or the end of the file.

```
Bromsgrove Hotel
Country house comfort between Worcester and
Birmingham.

A FAVOURITE WITH DINERS

As you step into the hallway of the Bromsgrove
Hotel, country house comfort welcomes you. On your
right you will see the original oak panelling and
fireplace with the sturdy staircase beyond. On
your left the friendly open comfort of the
reception, bar and restaurant beckon. Settle
yourself deeply in a sofa or armchair and enjoy a
drink before your meal. For guests in a hurry or
meeting casually there is also a tempting choice
of hot or cold bar meals.

The restaurant itself is full of character. High
backed, Moorish style chairs match the lattice
blue of the ceiling. The seats and tablecloths
reflect the springtime cherry blossom of the
garden and patio that the (restarant) overlooks.
Generous, beautifully cooked steaks, garden fresh
(vegatables) and a wide choice of hors d'oeuvres
from the country dresser are regular features of a
meal at the Bromsgrove Hotel.

DOWN TO BUSINESS

Many business people like to escape from the
office or sales calls and talk quietly in one of
the five reception rooms. The Houseman, Malvern,
Cedar, (grafton) and (clent) rooms can accommodate
meetings or receptions for up to 40 people. For
relaxation between (sesions) there is even a games
room and pool table upstairs.

STAYING THE NIGHT

All bedrooms have bath or shower, colour
television and tea and coffee making facilities.
Whether for (busines) or as a base for exploring
the surrounding countryside, the Bromsgrove Hotel
is the ideal comfortable hotel in which to stay.

The ivy covered hall with its solid oak front door
and latticed windows is attractively set back from
a curving driveway. The approach from the ample
car park takes you through the arched remains of
the old stable building.

Candidate number
Candidate name
```

Notes

You are given several instructions. To ensure that you carry all of them out, it might help you to jot them down first:

Identify and number each amendment in the sequence in which you should do them

1   Change Bromsgrove Hotel throughout the document to Bradshaw House Hotel. Use Search and Replace or similar facility if you have it.

2 Carry out the alterations to the text as indicated. There are 7 altogether, not counting the instruction to leave a correction as it is. Again, it might help you to remember to carry them all out if you number each one.

3 Identify and correct four spelling errors.

4 Change the line length to 65 characters. You should be able to tell by looking at the ruler line how many characters there are currently to the line.

5 Justify the right margin before printing out.

Task 2: Candidate's copy for Task 2

Open the file called INFHOTEL and make the corrections shown below. Four spelling errors have not been corrected – please check and correct them as well. Please alter Bromsgrove Hotel to Bradshaw House Hotel throughout the document. Change the printing line to 65 characters. Justify all paragraphs before printing a copy of the amended document.

> **Check carefully your print commands before printing out**

Two blank Lines here please

```
Bromsgrove Hotel
Country house comfort between Worcester and
Birmingham.

A FAVOURITE WITH DINERS

As you step into the hallway of the Bromsgrove
Hotel, country house comfort welcomes you. On your
right you will see the original oak panelling and
fireplace with the sturdy staircase beyond. On
your left the friendly open comfort of the
reception, bar and restaurant beckon. Settle
yourself deeply in a sofa or armchair and enjoy a
drink before your meal. For guests in a hurry or
meeting casually there is also a tempting choice
of hot or cold bar meals.
```
Stet   *δ*   *variety*

```
The restaurant itself is full of character. High
backed, Moorish style chairs match the lattice
blue of the ceiling. The seats and tablecloths
reflect the springtime cherry blossom of the
garden and patio that the restarant overlooks.
Generous, beautifully cooked steaks, garden fresh
vegatables and a wide choice of hors d'oeuvres
from the country dresser are regular features of a
meal at the Bromsgrove Hotel.
```
trs

```
DOWN TO BUSINESS

Many business people like to escape from the
office or sales calls and talk quietly in one of
the five reception rooms. The Houseman, Malvern,
Cedar, grafton and clent rooms can accommodate
meetings or receptions for up to 40 people. For
relaxation between sesions there is even a games
room and pool table upstairs.
```
uc/uc

```
STAYING THE NIGHT

All bedrooms have bath or shower, colour
television and tea and coffee making facilities.
Whether for busines or as a base for exploring
the surrounding countryside, the Bromsgrove Hotel
is the ideal comfortable hotel in which to stay.

The ivy covered hall with its solid oak front door
and latticed windows is attractively set back from
a curving driveway. The approach from the ample
car park takes you through the arched remains of
the old stable building.

Candidate number
Candidate name
```

In summer wedding guests gather happily on the lawn and patio which adjoin the large dining room.

TASK 3: TEXT AMENDMENT

Here is the second task requiring the candidate to recall a document and amend the text. Before you tackle this task, list the instructions first. Look carefully for the deliberate spelling mistakes and remember to reset the margin as instructed, before you print out. **Note**: The abbreviations in this Task are written out in full in another task.

Text for Task 3
Instructions to Tutor.

Set a left margin of 25 mm (1 inch) and a right hand margin which will give a line length of 60 characters.

The text and its layout must be followed exactly, although line endings may differ. Deliberate errors which have to be keyed in are marked with a circle on the text.

```
ELITE GROUP MARKETING AGENCY

Revised Material - Makepeace & Woodthorpe plc

        LIVLEY - INFORMED - PROVOCATIVE

Keeping up-to-date was never easy. Changes in law, technology,
management techniques and working practises all these are
happening daily. Yet the need to keep abreast has never been
greater. In today's economic climate managers and specialists
who really know what's going on have a distinct advantage.
Koolman cassette/compact disc bullitins are designed to give you
that advantage.

If time is the problem, the logical answer is better use of
wasted time. If you drive 20 000 miles a year you probably spend
the equivalent of around 10 working weeks behind the wheel. By
listening to Koolman cassette/compact disc bulletins you could
start to put that time to imediate use.

In the coming months MB will cover:

APPRAISAL INTERVEIWS - Five points that you must consider.

TIME PLANNING DIARIES - Does it need £150 to be spent to be
organised?

NEW TECHNOLOGY - A managers survival guide.

BOOK REVIEWS - Providing a summary of the latest books.


In recent issues PTB has investigated:

RECRUITMENT INTERVIEWING - Which alternatives to the interview
give better results?

COMPLACENCY IN TRAINING - What trainers can do to overcome it.
```

Task 3: Candidate's copy
Recall the file THREE. Amend the text as shown below correcting all errors. Type all abbreviations in the body of the text in full. Left margin of 37 mm (1½ inches).

ELITE GROUP MARKETING AGENCY

Revised Material - Makepeace & Woodthorpe plc

← ————————— LIVLEY - INFORMED - PROVOCATIVE

Keeping up-to-date was never easy. Changes in law, technology,
management techniques and working practises⌐ all these are
⁊ uc happening daily. ~~Yet~~ the need to keep abreast has never been
greater. In today's economic climate |managers⌐and|specialists, *trs*
who really know what's going on have a distinct advantage.
Koolman cassette/compact disc bullitins are designed to give you
that advantage.

If time is the problem, the logical answer is better use of
⁊ wasted time. ~~If you drive 20 000 miles a year you probably spend~~
~~the equivalent of around 10 working weeks behind the wheel.~~ By
listening to Koolman cassette/compact disc bulletins you could
start to put that time to imediate use.

In the coming months MB will cover:

APPRAISAL INTERVEIWS - Five points that you must consider.

TIME PLANNING DIARIES - Does it need £150 to be spent to be
organised?

NEW TECHNOLOGY - A managers survival guide.

BOOK REVIEWS - Providing a summary of the latest books.

In recent issues PTB has investigated:

RECRUITMENT INTERVIEWING - Which alternatives to the interview
give better results?

COMPLACENCY IN TRAINING - What trainers can do to overcome it.

NEW TECHNOLOGY AGREEMENTS — How one Co made it pay off.

NEGOTIATING - Four steps to getting your ideas accepted.

❝❞ Bear in mind the rules
for display when centring a
table vertically and
horizontally ❞❞

TASK 4: TABULATION

Here is another task where you are asked to create your own file and then in this case, to
key in a table and total up some figures.

Apply the rules that you will have learned in typewriting to calculate where you will have to
set your margins and tabs in order to centre the table horizontally. You will find it quicker
to work out the vertical centring after you have keyed in the table.

There is no need to use the automatic facility for double line spacing. In fact, in a Table
such as this, where you have to press the return at the end of every line anyway, you
might find it more convenient to press the return twice.

Work out the totals of the vertical columns, and double check these by adding the totals
horizontally as well. Use your calculator to check your final results. You would have about
15 to 20 minutes to do this task.

Task 4: Candidate's copy

Create a document called FOUR and set up a suitable format to centre the table below, horizontally and vertically on A4 paper. Complete the table by totalling the vertical columns and entering the totals in the last line. Save to disk and print a hard copy.

(31 marks)

```
            ELITE GROUP ESTATE AGENTS

            Sales of Property Type by Branch Office

                                   BRANCH OFFICE
            TYPE OF PROPERTY    BACKWELL    CLEVEDON    PORTISHEAD    TOTALS

     Type in  Terraced           2           4           3             9
     double   Semi-detached      10          4           11            25
     line     Detached           3           4           5             12
     spacing  Bungalows          1           -           2             3
              Maisonettes        -           -           2             2
              Flats              1           2           -             3


            TOTALS                                                     54
```

SEG KEYBD PAPER 2A GENERAL, WORD PROCESSING

TASK 5: FORM LETTER

In this examination the standard letter is keyed in, in advance, with numbered entry points. The candidate then recalls the letter and inserts the variable information as instructed.

When you prepare the letter, make sure that you delete the number at each entry point when you insert the variable data, and that you check the spacing afterwards. You would have approximately 15 minutes to do this Task.

Text for Task 5
Instructions to teacher.

Set a left-hand margin of 25 mm (1 inch) and a right-hand margin which will give a line length of 65 characters.

```
                    ELITE GROUP ESTATE AGENTS
                     Bristol Regional Offices
                       Great Western Road
                             Bristol
                             BS9 7BB

Ref (1)

(2)

(3)

Dear (4)

(5)

Thank you for your instructions to place the above property on
the market through our agency. Following my inspection on (6)
last, our printers are now in the process of preparing the house
particulars.

I expect to have the first proof from the printers by (7) and
look forward to showing these to you then.

In the meantime, should you have any further queries, please
contact me at our (8) office.

Yours sincerely
ELITE GROUP ESTATE AGENTS


(9)
Sales Negotiator
```

Task 5: Candidate's copy

Recall the form letter five used by the company to confirm the acceptance of instructions to sell a property. Complete the letter from the information given below. Save the document to disk and print a hard copy.

(1) JB/426

(2) Today's date

(3) Mrs A Roberts, 47 Edgar Close, Clevedon, Avon, BS21 6HF

(4) Mrs Roberts

(5) 29 Waterloo Avenue, Backwell, Avon, BS20 6PJ
    (Please print in caps)

(6) Thurs

(7) ~~Next~~ Monday, 21 June 1988

(8) Backwell

(9) John Bundy

MEG OSIP PAPER 2   ## TASK 6: LETTER COMPOSITION WITH MERGING OF TEXT

In this type of task it is necessary to refer to several documents. One of these documents would be stored before the examination on a database, and you would be expected to extract the relevant details, and then *merge* them with your text. As you are not required to include all the information, once the text is displayed on the screen, read the instructions again and check what items you should delete.

Text for Task 6
Instructions to Tutor.
Create a file called mc/6 and key in the text below:

DOT MATRIX PRINTERS

Ascot RT12	150.00 + VAT = 172.50
Ascot RT14	289.00 + VAT = 332.35
Ascot RT16	398.00 + VAT = 457.70
Ascot TT19	350.00 + VAT = 402.50
Ascot TS48	578.00 + VAT = 664.79
Ascot VX10	260.00 + VAT = 299.00
Golden Wand GW12/14	198.95 + VAT = 228.79
Golden Wand HT34C	228.95 + VAT = 263.29
Golden Wand HT44C	319.95 + VAT = 367.94
Golden Wand KSR14	189.95 + VAT = 218.44

THERMAL MATRIX PRINTERS

Sun SST90	129.95 + VAT = 149.44
Super Sun SST80	290.90 + VAT = 334.54
Super Sun SST1000	490.90 + VAT = 564.54

Task 6: Candidate's copy
Your firm has received the following letter:

```
123 Lewes Road
Macclesfield
Cheshire
SK11 6QY

12 October 1984

Birmingham Computer Centre
Aston House
Royal College Street
Birmingham
B5 4NJ


Dear Sirs

I have recently purchased a CBC Portable PC computer and am running a Modern Symphony
integrated package incorporating graphics, communication, spreadsheet, word processing and
database systems. I am using the computer and software package for freelance secretarial work
from home. My old typewriter/printer cannot handle the range of hard copy I now require and
I would be grateful if you would recommend a suitable printer.

I cannot afford to pay more than £250 for my printer but could offer my typewriter/printer,
an Everlast KSR, in part exchange if you take part exchanges. Any information you can supply
will be welcome.


Yours faithfully


Barbara Oliver (Miss)
```

> **Remember you will be expected to extract and delete some of the data stored on the file**

Compose a reply to Barbara Oliver from Birmingham Micro-computer Centre using the following information:

Thank her for her letter and say that she is probably already aware of the main disadvantages of her Everlast printer – it is daisywheel, slow and cannot handle graphics or colour. Advise her that although we do part exchanges we cannot offer her as much as she would probably get selling the machine privately. While we could offer her in the region of £75 subject to examination she could expect to get over £150 selling privately if the machine is in good condition. Bearing this in mind we advise her to sell her machine privately. Extract a list of machines in the £250 – £400 range from file mc/6. Tell her that all the machines on that list should meet her requirements and that they all have colour capability. Point out that they are all much quicker than a single element printer. All include cable and a suitable interface. Include leaflets on all the machines suggested and offer to assist her further once she has examined what we have sent. The letter is signed by the Sales Manager, Mr Robert Davidson.
Print out your reply.

Note
Details of the printers are contained on the file mc/6. Candidates are required to load this file and extract a list of the machines as instructed in the notes.

SEG KEYBD PAPER 2B EXTENDED WORD PROCESSING

TASKS 7 AND 8

This is another example of several tasks in an examination paper which are interdependent and where information contained on one file has to be inserted into another. In this case you are asked to compose a letter based partly on notes given to you and partly on information contained in a form which you had to complete previously. Finally a Table, which had to be recalled and amended in an earlier task, is merged into letter. Note that you are required to print *two* copies of the letter.

We present the Form Letter in Task 7 and the notes for the composition of the letter in Task 8.

TASK 7: FORM LETTER

In the examination, the form letter below must be keyed in, in advance, by the person responsible.

Text for Task 7
Instructions to teacher.

Set a left-hand margin of 25mm (1 inch) and a right-hand margin which will give a line length of 65 characters.

```
                          ELITE GROUP ESTATE AGENTS
                                Brunel House
                             Great Western Road
                                  BRISTOL
                                  BS9 7BB

(date)

ADVANCE DETAILS OF NEWLY AVAILABLE PROPERTY FOR SALE

Branch:

Property:

Full name of seller:

Price:

The above property has been taken on to the books of this
office for sale at the price shown.

Please check your list of potential buyers and telephone any
whom you think might be interested in this property.

Full printed details will be forwarded to you as soon as they
are available, however, a summary of the property is given
below:

Situation:        Detached/Semi-detached/Terraced/Maisonette

Reception rooms:  One/Two/Three/Four

Bedroms:          One/Two/Three/Four/Five/Six

Garage:           Yes/No

Gardens:          None/Small/Medium/Large/Well kept/Mature

Close to:         Schools/Shops/Bus Routes

The property will be sold with vacant possession and viewing
is by appointment with this office.



John Williams
Branch Manager
```

Task 7 Candidate's copy

Recall the file *TASK* which is a form letter used by the Elite Group Estate Agents branches to notify head office of the details of new property which they have taken onto their books for sale. Complete the form letter from the information given. Use today's date. Save the file to disk and print a hard copy.

ELITE GROUP ESTATE AGENTS
Brunel House
Great Western Road
BRISTOL
BS9 7BB

(date)

ADVANCE DETAILS OF NEWLY AVAILABLE PROPERTY FOR SALE

Branch: *PORTISHEAD*

Property: *8 Manor Close, Portishead, Avon, BS20 3PT*

Full name of seller: *Mrs Anne Roberts*

Price: *£47,550*

The above property has been taken on to the books of this
office for sale at the price shown.

Please check your list of potential buyers and telephone any
whom you think might be interested in this property.

Full printed details will be forwarded to you as soon as they
are available, however, a summary of the property is given
below:

Situation: ~~Detached~~/Semi-detached/~~Terraced~~/~~Maisonette~~

Reception rooms: One/(Two)/Three/Four

Bedrooms: One/Two/(Three)/Four/Five/Six

Garage: Yes/~~No~~

Gardens: None/Small/(Medium)/Large/(Well kept)/Mature

Close to: Schools/(Shops/Bus Routes)

The property will be sold with vacant possession and viewing
is by appointment with this office.

John Williams
Branch Manager

TASK 8: LETTER COMPOSITION

Using the information below and that given in Task 7, compose a letter to be sent to Mrs Roberts. Save the letter on disk under the file name Task 8. Print a hard copy.

A second copy of the letter is required. Mark this second copy 'For Backwell Office Files' in the right hand corner. Save this letter on disk under the file name Task 8A before it is printed.

Thank Mrs Roberts for the instructions to sell her property.

Inform her that the property will be offered for sale through all 6 Elite Group Estate Agents branches.

Mrs R. has requested details of any mortgage facilities which are available. Inform her of the newly arranged mortgages rates which have been negotiated with a leading building society.

Merge the amended table created in task two into the letter at this point.

End the letter by asking Mrs R to contact this office if she would like any further information about the mortgage scheme.

The letter will be signed by John Williams, the Branch Manager.

DISPLAYS

This section suggests ways of tackling the tasks, and presents displays of them all.

You will find a candidate's display of Tasks 1, 3, 5, 6, 7 and 8 and a Tutor's display of Tasks 2 and 4.

TEXT CREATION

TASK 1: CANDIDATE'S DISPLAY

Notes

There were 5 errors in the typescript all of which the candidate identified. These are labelled a) to e) in the display below.

Notice that the word 'intervals' had to be inserted between 'frequent' and 'and', not after 'really'.

Several marks would have been lost for the errors in spacing in the fourth paragraph and for failing to indent 5 spaces in the final section.

GENERAL NOTES ON CHARTERING

We have compiled these notes on chartering following requests from new
clients./We hope they are sufficiently comprehensive to be of use to /
seasoned dinghy sailors, perhaps sailing a yacht for the first time,
or similarly to boat owners, now chartering./We hope they are comprehensive
but your comments would be gratefully appreciated.

TAKE-OVER

The charterer should note where all gear, etc is stowed on board.
Particular attention should be paid to instructions given during
/demonstration on the use of all electrical, gas and mechanical
equipment.

FATIGUE

Many crews arrive for take-over after a long drive./It is a great
mistake to get under way without having a meal and a good rest.
Without these,/fatigue may set in and this will affect your judgement,
efficiency and the safety of the crew and yacht.

SEASICKNESS

Try to avoid anti-histamine tablets; they tend to make you sleepy.
The best tablets are Kwells, Stugeron or Maxaion./Avoid fatty foods
for a week/ before sailing./Take aerated drinks with you but no
alcohol./Eat dry biscuits at frequent intervals and suck glucose
sweets./If you really do suffer badly, do not go below, but stay in
the fresh air and fix your eyes on a point which is stationary.

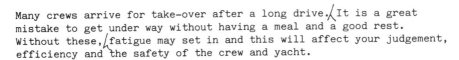

"Four errors in spacing
in this paragraph"

WHAT TO BRING

We will provide cooking utensils, crockery, cleaning materials and
toilet paper./Freshly laundered sleeping bags are available for hire.
You will need to bring:

     At least 2 sets of warm clothing
     Sensible deck shoes
     Good quality wet weather gear
     Food and drink
     Suntan oil

"This paragraph should
have been indented 5 spaces,
not 3"

TASK 2: TEXT AMENDMENT; A TUTOR'S DISPLAY

Notes

Five instructions were identified. Do Instruction 1 first and 5 last. The other 3 you could do in any order:

1 **Change** Bromsgrove Hotel to Bradshaw House Hotel throughout the document. You would be expected to use the automatic search and replace facility. It would be advisable to do this first. Otherwise if you used the facility to change the name of the hotel after you had typed the original heading in capitals, it would not be automatically replaced.

2 Carry out the **7 amendments**, taking care not to alter the word 'choice' to 'variety'. Here are some suggestions on how to do them, although you may have to modify them a little according to the system you use. The letters cross-refer to the changes on the display:

   a) Type the heading (it should now be 'Bradshaw House Hotel') in capitals. Either use the *overtype* facility if you have it, or *delete the line* first.

   b) *Insert* 2 blank lines by pressing RETURN twice.

   c) *Move* the paragraph. Remember to move the line space below the paragraph as well, and to check that you have the correct number of line spaces above and below it in the new position.

d) *Delete the sentence.* Most systems will have a quick way of doing this – avoid pressing the delete key character by character!

e) Transpose the two words. The quickest way to do this is to *remove and save* (or copy and cut) one of the words and then paste it in the correct position.

f) Change to upper case – use *overtype* if you have it.

g) Key in the new paragraph in place of the one you have moved. Check at the same time that your line spacing is correct.

3 Identify and correct the **four spelling errors**.

You would probably find it easier to locate the spelling errors on the hard copy you are given, rather than from the screen. (In an examination, of course, you would not have seen the teacher's copy with the errors clearly ringed!)

4 **Change the line length** to 65 characters.

A 50 space typing line was used, with the left margin 1½ inches in. To extend the line by 15 spaces you will have to move the left margin 5 spaces to the left and the right 10 spaces to the right.

5 **Justify** the right margin.

Make sure your cursor is at the *top* of the document before giving the command to justify. If your system allows you to, check that you have given this command correctly, as you are not allowed to print out a second time.

 BRADSHAW HOUSE HOTEL

Country house comfort between Worcester and Birmingham,

 The ivy covered Hall with its solid oak front door and latticed windows is attractively set back from a curving driveway, The approach from the ample car park takes you through the arched remains of the old stable building,

A FAVOURITE WITH DINERS

As you step into the hallway of the Bradshaw House Hotel, country house comfort welcomes you, On your right you will see the original oak panelling and fireplace with the sturdy staircase beyond, On your left the friendly open comfort of the reception, bar and restaurant beckon, For guests in a hurry or meeting casually there is also a tempting choice of hot or cold bar meals,

 The restaurant itself is full of character, High backed, Moorish style chairs match the lattice blue of the ceiling, The seats and tablecloths reflect the springtime cherry blossom of the garden and patio that the restaurant overlooks, Generous, beautifully cooked steaks, fresh garden vegetables and a wide choice of hors d'oeuvres from the country dresser are regular features of a meal at the Bromsgove Hotel,

DOWN TO BUSINESS

Many business people like to escape from the office or sales calls and talk quietly in one of the five reception rooms, The Houseman, Malvern, Cedar, Grafton and Clent rooms can accommodate meetings or receptions for up to 40 people, For relaxation between sessions there is even a games room and pool table upstairs,

STAYING THE NIGHT

All bedrooms have bath or shower, colour television and tea and coffee making facilities, Whether for business or as a base for exploring the surrounding countryside, the Bradshaw House Hotel is the ideal comfortable hotel in which to stay,

 In summer, wedding guests gather happily on the lawn and patio which adjoin the large dining room,

Candidate number
Candidate name

TASK 3: TEXT AMENDMENT; CANDIDATE'S DISPLAY

Notes

In this display, the candidate followed all the instructions correctly and identified the 8 errors (which are ringed on the copy of the text which had to be keyed in beforehand).

Although the left margin was positioned half an inch in, as instructed, marks would have been lost for not including the heading. (The cursor should have been placed above it when the margin was repositioned).

All the abbreviations were typed in full, except for two. In the examination, this task was the last of 6, and as the abbreviations are written in full in the first task, it needs a good memory and a cool head in the pressures of the examination room to remember where they were!

A candidate who thought of looking in other parts of the paper would have also found help in spelling some of the words, such as bulletin.

❝❝ The cursor should have been on the line above the heading when the margin was moved ❞❞

```
ELITE GROUP MARKETING AGENCY

Revised Material - Makepeace & Woodthorpe plc

LIVELY - INFORMED - PROVOCATIVE

Keeping up-to-date was never easy. Changes in law,
technology, management techniques and working
practices - all these are happening daily. The
need to keep abreast has never been greater. In
today's economic climate specialists and managers
who really know what is going on have a distinct
advantage. Koolman cassette/compact disc bulletins
are designed to give you that advantage.

If time is the problem, the logical answer is
better use of wasted time. By listening to
Koolman cassette/compact disc bulletins you could
start to put that time to immediate use.

In recent issues PTB has investigated:

RECRUITMENT INTERVIEWING - Which alternatives to
the interview give better results?

COMPLACENCY IN TRAINING - What trainers can do to
overcome it.

NEW TECHNOLOGY AGREEMENTS - How one company made
it pay off.

NEGOTIATING - Four steps to getting your ideas
accepted.

In the coming months MB will cover:

APPRAISAL INTERVIEWS - Five points that you must
consider.

TIME PLANNING DIARIES - Does it need #150 to be
spent to be organised?

NEW TECHNOLOGY - A manager's survival guide.

BOOK REVIEWS - Providing a summary of the latest
books.
```

❝❝ Two extra spaces were left here when the sentence was deleted – a very common error which could be avoided. ❞❞

❝❝ The abbreviations should have been written out in full ❞❞

TASK 4: TABULATION; A TUTOR'S DISPLAY

Use a calculator to check your figures

Here is the display of the Table where the columns had to be totalled. With approximately only 15 minutes to do this task you would need to carry out the calculations for layout and the totalling of the columns as quickly as possible.

```
ELITE GROUP ESTATE AGENTS


Sales of Property Type by Branch Office

                     BRANCH OFFICE
TYPE OF PROPERTY     BACKWELL    CLEVEDON    PORTISHEAD    TOTALS

Terraced                2           4            3            9

Semi-detached          10           4           11           25

Detached                3           4            5           12

Bungalows               1           -            2            3

Maisonettes             -           -            2            2

Flats                   1           2            -            3
                     _____

TOTALS                 17          14           23           54
```

TASK 5: FORM LETTER; CANDIDATE'S DISPLAY

Notes

This display is almost perfect. The candidate deleted the numbers and inserted the entries at the correct points. A mark would have been lost for the only error – which at least was consistent!

If you accidentally delete some of the text in a document such as this, where you do not have a hard copy to refer to, remember that if you have time you can always abandon your document and recall the original form letter if your system allows you to do this.

```
                        ELITE GROUP ESTATE AGENTS
                          Bristol Regional Offices
                            Great Western Road
                                 Bristol
                                 BS9 7BB


            Ref:  JB/426

            23 May 1988

            Mrs A Roberts
            47 Edgar Close
            CLEVEDON
            Avon
            BS21 6HF

            Dear Mrs Roberts

            29 WATERLOO AVENUE, BLACKWELL, AVON, BS21 6PJ

            Thank you for your instructions to place the above property on
            the market through our agency. Following my inspection on
            Thursday last, our printers are now in the process of
            preparing the house particulars.
```

This should have been Backwell

I expect to have the first proof from the printers by Monday,
21 June 1988 and look forward to showing these to you then.

In the meantime, should you have any further queries, please
contact me at our Blackwell office.

Yours sincerely
ELITE GROUP ESTATE AGENTS

John Bundy
Sales Negotiator

TASK 6: LETTER COMPOSITION WITH MERGING OF TEXT; CANDIDATE'S DISPLAY

Notes
This is a good answer. All the points have been made in correct English. There is only one
error in the typing – Encs was omitted. However, marks would have been lost for failing to
extract the relevant details about the printers – only those in the price range of £250 to
£400 should have been listed.

You would not of course have the details in front of you. The *full* list has to be accessed
and inserted in the letter and then those selling at less than £250 and more than £400
should be deleted, leaving 7 in all.

                              Birmingham Computer Centre   **Name of company**
                                      Aston House   **would be more effective in**
                                 Royal College Street   **capitals**
                                     BIRMINGHAM
                                       B5 4NJ

8 March 1989

Miss B Oliver
123 Lewes Road
MACCLESFIELD
Cheshire
SK11 6QY

Dear Miss Oliver

Thank you for letter of 12 October 1984 explaining to us about your
present printer which is unable to to handle the type of material you
require from your present software. As you are probably aware your own
printer is a daisywheel printer which is very slow and is unable to
handle graphics and colour.

We can offer you a part exchange on your present printer in the region
of £75 subject to an examination but we feel that if you sold it
privately you would expect to get in the region of over £150 if it is in
a good condition.

Listed below are a number of printers which fall within a price range of
between £250 – £400 each of these have the capacity required including
colour and each of them are much quicker than your present printer.
Each comes with a cable and a suitable interface for your computer:

```
DOT MATRIX PRINTERS

Ascot RT12              150.00 + VAT = 172.50
Axcot RT15              289.00 + VAT = 332,35

Golden Wand GW12/14     198.95 + VAT = 228.79
Golden Wand HT34C       228.95 + VAT = 263.29
Golden Wand HT44C       319.95 + VAT = 367.94
Golden Wand KS14        189.95 + VAT = 218.44

THERMAL MATRIX PRINTERS

Sun SST90               129.95 + VAT = 149.44
Super Sun SST80         290.90 + VAT = 334.54
```

66 The printers priced under £250 and over £400 should have been deleted, while Ascot VX10 at £299 should have been included 99

```
7 March 1989

Miss B Oliver


I enclose leaflets on each of these printers and if I can be of any
further assistance please do not hesitate to telephone or write to me
about any of these printers.

I look forward to hearing from you in the near future.

Yours sincerely



Robert Davidson
Sales Manager
```

66 'Encs' was omitted 99

TASK 7: FORM LETTER; CANDIDATE'S DISPLAY

Notes

The candidate did not use overtype when completing the form, but since, in this case, the entries were single line, it was not necessary. However, after keying in the first entry, the candidate pressed the return instead of using the cursor movement keys to reach the next entry point and so inadvertently inserted an extra line space in the form.

The deletions in the second part of the form have been done quite well. There is no quick way of deleting characters in the middle of a 'string' of characters (word processing systems do not generally recognise separate words, as such, when they are linked by a stroke) and in the pressure of an examination, it is quite easy to delete too many or, as in this case, too few of the characters.

It is important to delete any unwanted items, since penalties are usually just as high for including extra words as they are for excluding them.

```
                    ELITE GROUP ESTATE AGENTS
                          Brunel House
                       Great Western Road
                            BRISTOL
                            BS9 7BB


26 May 1988

ADVANCE DETAILS OF NEWLY AVAILABLE PROPERTY FOR
SALE                                              ❝❝ Error in the spelling of
                                                      the town ❞❞
Branch: PORTSHEAD



Property: 8 Manor Close, Portishead, Avon BS20 3PT

Full name of seller: Mrs Anne Roberts        ❝❝ Extra line space. Avoid
                                               pressing the return (or space
Price: #47,550                                  bar) when skimming over
                                                       text ❞❞
The above property has been taken on to the books
of this office for sale at the price shown.

Please check your list of potential buyers and
telephone any whom you think might be interested
in this property.

Full printed details will be forwarded to you as
soon as they are available, however, a summary of
the property is given below:

Situation: Semi-detached○
                                        ❝❝ Deletions omitted ❞❞
Reception rooms: Two

Bedrooms: Three
Garage: Yes

Gardens: Medium /Well kept

Close to: Schools/Shops/Bus routes

The property will be sold with vacant possession
and viewing is by appointment with this office.

John Williams
Branch Manager
```

TASK 8: LETTER COMPOSITION

Notes

All the points which should have been made, have been included in the letter.

The second paragraph is weak in that it repeats the instructions word for word. However, the candidate did make use of the information in the form to mention that advance details had been sent out.

More initiative is shown in the third paragraph, with a nice touch in the final paragraph, where the writer returns to the opening sentence. Omission of the date would have lost marks.

The Table of Mortgage Rates which had to be amended in an earlier task, was successfully recalled and merged into the letter.

Note that a hard copy of this letter had to be printed out and saved and then a second disk copy made and altered accordingly before printing.

```
                    ELITE GROUP ESTATE AGENTS
                          Brunel House
                      Great Western Road
                            BRISTOL
                            BS9 7BB

A fictitious organisation for examination purposes
only

Ref JW/cr

Mrs Anne Roberts                               66 Date was omitted 99
8 Manor Close
PORTISHEAD
Avon
BS20 3PT

Dear Mrs Roberts

8 MANOR CLOSE, PORTISHEAD

Thank you for instructing us to sell your property
at the above address.

We shall be offering your property for sale
through all six of our Elite Group Estate Agents
Branches, and have already sent advance details
out to them.

I understand that you would like details of any
mortgage facilities which are available, and I am       66 Spelling error 99
pleased to inform that we have recently negotited
new rates with a leading building society as
follows:

Monthly repayment Rates at 11% Per Annum
```

AMOUNT OF MORTGAGE	LENGTH OF LOAN 10 YEARS	15 YEARS	20 YEARS	25 YEARS
1 000	18.75	12.50	9.35	7.50
5 000	93.75	62.50	46.75	37.50
10 000	187.50	125.00	93.50	75.00
20 000	375.00	250.00	187.00	150.00
50 000	937.50	625.00	467.50	375.00

```
These rates in no way constitute a formal contract
and are subject to the usual status conditions of
applicants being met.

The rates quoted are valid until 31 December 1988.
```

2

Mrs Anne Roberts

If you would like any further information about
the mortgage scheme, our office will be glad to
help you.

I shall of course be in contact with you over the
sale of your property, but if in the meantime you
have any queries, please do not hesitate to
contact me at this office

Yours sincerely

Full stop omitted

John Williams
Branch Manager

11

GETTING STARTED

PUTTING IT ALL TOGETHER

ASSIGNMENT A

ASSIGNMENT B

ASSIGNMENT C

Mention has already been made about the *thematic* approach to writing GCSE examination papers and coursework assignments.

Because candidates for GCSE text processing examinations are being tested for more than mere proficiency in operating a keyboard, questions and tasks are written in such a way that the student is required to refer to other sources of information. Such information may appear in the preamble to, or in other parts of, the question paper or coursework assignment. In the case of coursework, the student may have to refer to reference material *outside* that provided by the Examining Board.

This last chapter gives you an opportunity to study, and perhaps work through, some of these **integrated tasks**.

INTEGRATED TASKS

You work in the office of Millhouse School, Longton Road, Guildford, Surrey, GU1 4XJ. The following are tasks you may be required to undertake in your capacity as a clerk/typist.

Task 1   Copy of Health and Safety Code of Practice.
Task 2   New telephone numbers list.
Task 3   Letter to parents.
Task 4   Duty Rota.
Task 5   Advertisement and covering letter - staff vacancy.

TASK 1

Type a copy of the following using single line spacing for the main part of the document and double line spacing for the itemised list.
Use A4 paper and suitable equal margins.
The heading is HEALTH & SAFETY CODE OF PRACTICE.

Millhouse has compiled a detailed 'Statement of Organisation and Arrangements' (Code of Practice). This statement deals fully with all aspects of school safety. It does not replace the Local Authority's safety policy but is additional to it.

Copies of the Code of Practice are to be found in the school office and in the common room. Additional copies may be obtained from the Headteacher if required.

It has been written for teaching staff, non-teaching staff and students. All members of staff are required to familiarise themselves with its contents particularly in regard to:

a) their duties as employees
b) the role of the school's Health & Safety Officer
c) the special responsibilities held by some staff

stet

d) the obligations of all class teachers, particularly in the supervision of students

trs.

e) the provision of first-aid
f) emergency procedures, including the evacuation of premises in the event of fire.

TASK 2

Please arrange under the following shoulder headings :

Senior Staff (SS)
Administration (A)
Departments (D)
Support Services + Outside agencies (Sp Ss)
Year Heads (YH)

Single line-spacing. shoulder headings in bl. capitals and u/s.

MILLHOUSE SCHOOL TELEPHONE NUMBERS – from January 1990

123	School Office (A)	143	Head of SIXTH FORM (YH)
124	Head – P. M. Wetherell (SS)	144	Co-ordinator – Science (SS)
125	School Office – Internal (A)	145	Head of FIRST YEAR (YH)
126	Deputy Heads – K. O'Donnell,	146	P.E. Boys and Girls (D)
	G. L. Wood (SS)	147	Head of CDT (D)
127	Deputy Head – J. T. Stratford (SS)	148	English (D)
128	Science Prep. Room – Technicians (A)	149	Humanities (D)
129	Music Room (D)	150	Senior Teacher/Examinations
130	TVEI Co-ordinator (D)		Secretary (SS)
131	Main Reception Desk Switchboard (A)	151	Modern Languages (D)
132	Science Teachers' Room (A)	152	Library (Sp Ss)
133	Head's Secretary (A)	153	Mathematics (D)
134	Medical Room (Sp Ss)	154	MODEM – Computer Room (Sp Ss)
135	~~TVEI Business Centre/Head of~~ Business Education (D)	155	Pre-Vocational Office (D)
		156	Home Economics (D)
136	Reprographics Room (A)	157	Community Office (Sp Ss)
137	Staffroom (A)	158	Caretaker (Sp Ss)
138	Special needs (D)	159	MODEM Library Classroom (Sp Ss)
139	Millhouse NACRO Team (Sp Ss)	164	Head of SECOND YEAR and Head of
140	Art (D)		FIFTH YEAR (YH) (YH)
141	CDT Wood & Metal Stores (D)	165	Senior Tutor/Head of THIRD YEAR
142	Head of FOURTH YEAR (YH)	166	Community Co-ordinator (SS)

TASK 3

Type a draft of the following circular letter to parents. Copies of this letter will be printed on the school's headed paper so please leave at least 2″ (50mm) at the top of the A4 sheet.

Use the month and year only for the date, and address the letter – 'TO Parents/Guardians of all students'.

Dear Parent/Guardian

¶ As the end of term approaches, I take ~~the~~ this opportunity ~~to write to~~ of informing you of several important matters.

1. School Orchestra: This grows in strength + expertise. We had a very (succesful) — check spelling! concert a few weeks ago + are now planning a trip to Germany for next term — more details later.

2. Subject Teachers' Evenings: As you know we hold 2 evenings each yr when parents of each year group can come along + ? discuss their childs_ progress with the subject teachers. I hope you find these evenings as useful ¶ as the staff + I do. It is ~~heartening~~ encouraging to see so
NP many of you on these occasions. [Next term
Figs. we shall have evenings for parents of 1st + 4th yr students.

3. PTA Fund Raising: My sincere thanks to you all for the support given to the flourishing Parent/ Teachers Association. Whilst the school appreciates the time + ~~effort~~ given to fund raising, I would like to encourage wider participation in the
Stet ~~organization~~ running of the school + hv arranged a special meeting for early next term to put suggestions to you.

last yr you raised over £800 from a sponsered walk

The approaching holiday is one wh. it is hoped both staff + students can relax and enjoy a well-earned rest. However, students preparing
UC for public examinations next term wl need to spend some of their holidays preparing for these examinations. I know we can count on your support + encouragement in this matter.

Yours sinc.

(? print name)
Headteacher

TASK 4

Type the following duty rota centralizing the information vertically and horizontally and ruling as indicated in the draft. Use A4 paper.

~~SYSTEM~~

DUTY ~~ROTA~~   *stet*

Duty Day	Leader	2 i/c	Reserve Day
MONDAY	K. O'Donnell	P. Brown	THURSDAY
TUESDAY	G.L. Wood	J. Walls	FRIDAY
WEDNESDAY	J.T. Stratford	P. Hayes	MONDAY
THURSDAY	C. Jordan	M. Wood	TUESDAY
FRIDAY	R. Foxhill	R. Truman	WEDNESDAY

TEAMS

Leader : K. O'Donnell
Day : Monday

S. Stove
P. West,
F. Williams
P. Francome
A. Hunt
P. Brown

Leader : G.L. Wood
Day : Tuesday

N. Pike
V. Barton
T. Wills
F. Jones
B. Griffiths
J. Walls

Leader : J.T. Stratford
Day : Wednesday

S. Asher
V. Patel
J. Hennesey
I. Luver
C. Sharp
P. Hayes

Leader : C. Jordan
Day : Thursday

P. Crossier
D. Sanzogni
M. Bari
J. Nicholls
B. Stevens
M. Wood

Leader : R. Foxhill
Day : Friday

G. Armley
A. Wilcox
I. Childs
J. Poldark
A. Postlethwaite
J. Singh
R. Truman

TASK 5

Millhouse has a vacancy for a teacher of French to join a strong and flourishing Modern Languages Department. Ability to teach some German would be an advantage. The post is available from September next.

a) Compose and type a suitable advertisement for insertion in a newspaper. The space utilized should not exceed 4″ × 4″ (100 mm × 100 mm approx.)

Besides the above information ask candidates to send to the Headteacher (quote full address) for further details and an application form. Mention that the closing date for applications is 20 April.

b) Compose and type a letter to The Courier newspaper (address High Street, Guildford, Surrey, GU2 6BD) asking them to insert the advertisement in their Situations Vacant section on three consecutive evenings commencing 4th April.

Use the school's headed paper, take a carbon copy and address an envelope to the addressee.

2> ASSIGNMENT B

TASK 1

Type the following letter on A4 paper, correcting where necessary. Use the reference OP/Your initials, and today's date.

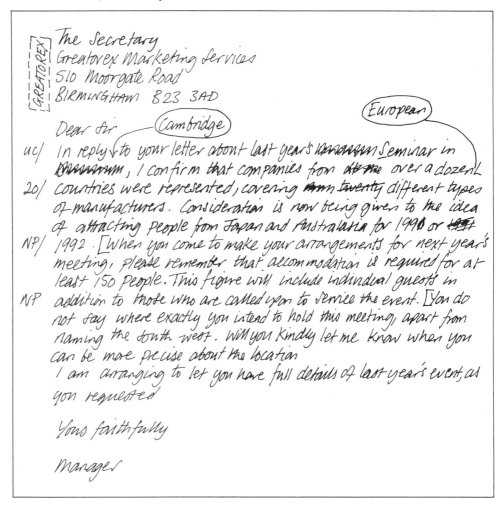

TASK 2

Correct the following typescript and display it exactly as shown.

```
                             ┌Northern
ENROLMENT DETAILS: │AREA MANAGERS MEETING
                          ┌our previous ANNUAL      (rate)
IMPORTANT: Past participants in ┤earlier GROUP MARKETING
SEMINARS are offered a specially reduced subscription┌of
£72.50. Be sure to mention this when you register!    ┴

Meeting No              298945/91/2/3

Location                Grand Eastern Hotel
                        Y O R K
                                     19
Registration            Wednesday 20 September 1990
                        from 1300 to 1630 hours
```

```
                                     Thursday 20
          Starting time             Friday 21 September 0930 hrs — in full!

                                     Friday   21      1600
          Ending time               Saturday 22 September 1700 hrs

          Language                   English

          Participation fees         Members £75.00
                                     Past participants £72.50
                                     Non-members £78.50

          To enrol                   Complete application form at the
                                     foot of the accompanying leaflet
```

                                                                    we are
Although hotel accommodation is not included in the fee, /
~~CROWN MARKETING~~ is prepared to arrange individual
accommodation in a limited number of guest rooms which
are being held locally for members and past participants.
A pre-addressed hotel form will accompany your acceptance
of registration. Please use this form when making your
reservation to ensure that your ~~are~~ handled promptly and
that you wil benefit from the rate.

reservation (left margin)

special delegate   *reservation is*

TASK 3

Type the following memo, using today's date.

```
MEMORANDUM                    AREA MANAGERS, POLICY CHANGE


TO   Finance Officer                         DATE   30 June 19..

FROM  Director                               REF    JE/MO/3

London/South East    Mr J E Mortensen        £3 500
South West           Mr A Drake
Midlands             Mr D J Prestwich         £1 500
North East           Mr ~~W Hodgkinson~~ ←————————— E. Pangloss
North West           Mr N F Fallowes          £1 000
Scotland             Mr F A S Hartley         £1 000
```

As you know, consideration has been given by the Board to the idea of switching round our regional managers. A decision has now been taken in favour of this policy and I list below the new pairings (managers and areas) which will operate from 1 October next. Our men will be informed of ~~this decision~~ these changes immediately. In some cases, a salary increase is called for and I have shown the appropriate increase against the rep. in question.

in full!

TASK 4

Correct the following typescript and display it exactly as shown.

NORTHERN AREA MANAGERS MEETING

Thursday and Friday 20 & 21 September 1990

MEETING OBJECTIVES

Aimed at the practising manager, this comprehensive two-day
programme with Arthur Browne and John Wilkinson leading,
is organised with the following points in mind:

1   to help all participants analyse their own leadershipstyle
    and performance over the past year
2   to present 'The Nineties Manager', the short title
    for modern leadership and goal settings effectively
3   to train all participants in how to develop
    their own leadership skills and to help them to encourage
    carry along their juniors.

All staff managers who are responsible for administration,
training, management development and personnel, will also
benefit from the meeting.

Enrolment details are given on the attached sheet.

- -

APPLICATION FORM (to be completed and sent to Mr E Major,
                  225 Grosvenor Avenue,
                  MANCHESTER, M29 2PQ, by 15 July 1990)

NAME ....POSITION...............

COMPANY ....

ADDRESS ....POSTCODE ....

CHEQUE ENCLOSED £........ (for ... participants)

TELEPHONE NO (Home .... (Company) ....

SIGNATURE ....

TYPE OF INDUSTRY ....

TASK 5

An A5 memo sheet should be used for the following.

"Jean, It would appear that there is growing support in some branches (notably Birmingham and Manchester) for further development of our Sports Societies, in particular the setting-up of competitions for Badminton, Tennis, Snooker and Table Tennis. Inter-branch competition already exists for Golf and we have an annual outing to Gleneagles. Please prepare a memo covering these points and ask that each of the Sports Secretaries make enquiries in their branches and pass back information to Head Office by 31 July at the latest. If the response is encouraging, we will collate replies and let branches know in September. By the way, if other sporting activities come to mind, these should be put forward for consideration." (The Director – John Holmes – is speaking to his Secretary – Jean Chang. Prepare the appropriate memo addressed to all branch managers.)

TASK 6

Type the following on A4 paper, avoiding the abbreviations where necessary. Do not cramp the account.

Dear Wendy   I have prepared the figures for the Company's Sports Club Income & Expenditure A/c for the year ending 31 March 1990, and I hope you will type this (in our usual format) and send out to all members in time for the AGM on 30 June.

Income	Subscriptions: Ladies	105		
	Gentlemen	190	295	
	Competition fees		385	
	Profit on functions		122	
	Donation		50	852
Expenditure	Printing and Stationery		273	
	Competition prizes		156	
	Postages etc		73	
	Affiliation fees		290	
	Surplus of Income over Expenditure		60	852

I will let you have the Agenda for the A-G-M very shortly.

Yours sincerely

Finance Officer

3 > ASSIGNMENT C

You are Secretary to Mr Richard Mortimer, one of the Partners in Bliss Leisure Holidays, a firm which specialises in the letting of holiday homes and the development of leisure centres in the UK and abroad.

TASK 1

Mr Mortimer will be going to France to visit two new developments on the west coast in the final weekend of next month. He will be going by car and plans to travel overnight on Friday on the car ferry from Portsmouth to Le Havre.

He has an appointment with M Honorat, the agent for Les Ombrees development at 4 pm on Saturday at the Grand Hotel in Dinard, where he will be staying the night. He will drive to Nantes on Sunday to meet the agent M Rochet in the afternoon at the site (Les Bagnols). He will be staying at the Atlantic Hotel on Sunday, returning to Portsmouth on the Monday night.

Mr Mortimer has asked you to look up the time of the night sailings for the Portsmouth/Le Havre car ferry, and to prepare an itinerary for his journey, using the 24 hour clock.

TASK 2

Mr Mortimer is thinking of getting a fax machine installed at his home, and has asked you to find the names and details of two leading suppliers who have a local office, which could provide back up service, supplies etc. Use the *Yellow Pages* to find the name and address and telephone number of two local agents acting for different manufacturers of fax machines. Type a memo to Mr Mortimer giving him this information.

TASK 3

The following telephone message has been received while Mr Mortimer was attending a meeting. Mr Mortimer has asked you compose a letter in reply to Robert Hunt, using the notes he has given you. Take a carbon copy of the letter, which will be signed by Richard Mortimer.

```
                    TELEPHONE  MESSAGF
For    Richard Mortimer              Date        (todays)

Name of caller    Robert Hunt        Time        10.00

Firm/address   Relion Developers Ltd,   Tel No    Bristol 81654
61 Weston Avenue, BRistol.            Extn        23
BS6 2No

Mr Hunt is anxious to know how the proposals for the development of
the S.W. Leisure Centre are getting on. He'd be grateful if
you could drop him a line as he will be away until early next
week.
```

Notes

Thank him for calling; apologise for my not being able to speak to him when he rang. Tell him that planning application has been made with the local Borough Council for the following main proposals: 200 berth marina with yacht servicing facilities and 20000 sq ft of leisure space (not 25000 as was originally proposed). The council will be meeting later this month and the prospects of the application being passed look good. We shall let him have the results as soon as these are available. Head the letter the South West Leisure Centre.

TASK 4

The list of current developments and the local agents in France needs updating. You have been asked to rearrange it in alphabetical order according to the location the development is situated.

Retype the list so that the location of the development is in the first column in alphabetical order, with the name of the development in the second and the agent in the third as shown the example below:

ARLES   Motte Les Bains   Suzanne Maurel

LIST OF AGENTS AND DEVELOPMENTS IN FRANCE

Francois Baptiste	Parc la Rouche	MONTPELLIER
Pierre Mathias	Chateau de Musson	TOURS
Suzanne Maurel	Motte Les Bains	ARLES
Alain Raye	Jardin de Rosat	ORANGE
Philippe Roget	Le Petit Arc	LOCHES
Simone Salon	Les Beaux Etangs	BIARRITZ

Please include the two new developments that I'll be seeing and their agents in Dinard and Nantes. Also the Vieux Moulin and Beaulieu both in Nimes. Agent is Jean Lexon.

BEAULIEU

INDEX

REVISE GUIDES

GCSE

TO HELP YOU ORGANISE YOUR WORKLOAD

REVISION

FOR THE COUNTDOWN TO GCSE.

PLANNER

WEEK   DATE   TARGET

4 FOUR		
3 THREE		
2 TWO		
1 ONE		

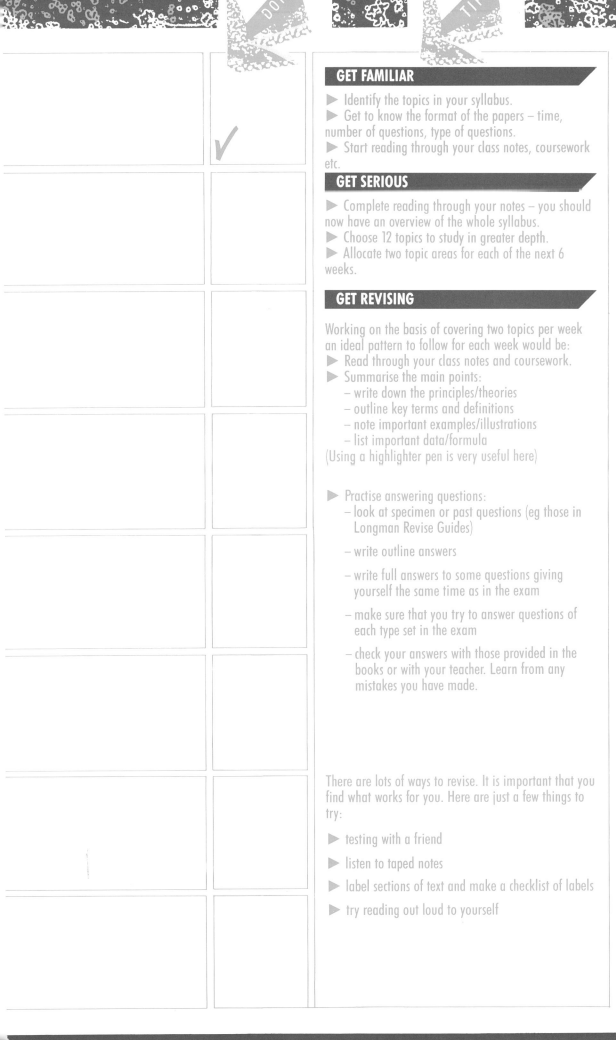

GET FAMILIAR

▶ Identify the topics in your syllabus.
▶ Get to know the format of the papers – time, number of questions, type of questions.
▶ Start reading through your class notes, coursework etc.

GET SERIOUS

▶ Complete reading through your notes – you should now have an overview of the whole syllabus.
▶ Choose 12 topics to study in greater depth.
▶ Allocate two topic areas for each of the next 6 weeks.

GET REVISING

Working on the basis of covering two topics per week an ideal pattern to follow for each week would be:
▶ Read through your class notes and coursework.
▶ Summarise the main points:
  – write down the principles/theories
  – outline key terms and definitions
  – note important examples/illustrations
  – list important data/formula
(Using a highlighter pen is very useful here)

▶ Practise answering questions:
  – look at specimen or past questions (eg those in Longman Revise Guides)

  – write outline answers

  – write full answers to some questions giving yourself the same time as in the exam

  – make sure that you try to answer questions of each type set in the exam

  – check your answers with those provided in the books or with your teacher. Learn from any mistakes you have made.

There are lots of ways to revise. It is important that you find what works for you. Here are just a few things to try:

▶ testing with a friend

▶ listen to taped notes

▶ label sections of text and make a checklist of labels

▶ try reading out loud to yourself

GET RESULTS

WEEK	DATE	TARGET
12 TWELVE		
11 ELEVEN		
10 TEN		
9 NINE		
8 EIGHT		
7 SEVEN		
6 SIX		
5 FIVE		

USING THE PLANNER — GET STARTED

▶ Begin on week 12. The reverse side of the planner covers weeks 12 – 5 and this side covers weeks 4 – 1 – the countdown to the exams.

▶ Use a calendar to put dates onto your planner and write in the dates of your exams.

▶ Use the suggestions alongside each week of the planner.

▶ Fill in your targets for each day and try to stick to them. If not, remember to re-schedule for another time.

▶ If you start using the planner less than 12 weeks before your exam try to include the suggestions for those weeks you missed, don't try to catch everything up at once. Spread the tasks fairly evenly over the weeks remaining.

√

GET CONFIDENCE

▶ Have a final read through of all your class notes and coursework.
▶ Read through the summaries you have already made.
▶ Try to reduce these summary notes to a single sheet of A4.
▶ Test yourself to check that you can remember everything on each A4 page.
▶ Go over the practice questions already attempted.
▶ Try to visit the place where the exams are to be held. This will help you to feel more familiar with the setting.

THE DAY BEFORE – GET SET

▶ Read through each A4 summary sheet for your 12 topic areas.
▶ Check that you have all the equipment you need for the exam.
▶ Do something you enjoy in the evening.
▶ Go to bed reasonably early. Tired students rarely give their best.

THE EXAM – GET UP AND GO

▶ Have a good breakfast to give you energy.
▶ Don't panic – everyone else is nervous too.
▶ Remember, the examiners are looking for opportunities to give you marks, not take them away!